The Church in the Power
of the Spirit

The Church in the Power of the Spirit

Keswick 2006

Edited by Ali Hull

Authentic

LONDON ● ATLANTA ● HYDERABAD

Keswick
ministries
bringing the Word alive

First published in 2006 by Authentic Media
9 Holdom Avenue, Bletchley, Milton Keynes, Bucks., MK1 1QR
285 Lynnwood Avenue, Tyrone, GA 30290, USA
OM Authentic Media, Medchal Road, Jeedimetla Village,
Secunderabad 500 055, A.P., India

Authentic Media is a division of Send the Light Ltd., a company limited by
guarantee (registered charity no. 270162)

British Library Cataloguing in Publication Data
A catalogue record for this book is available from
the British Library

ISBN-13: 978-1-85078-720-4
ISBN-10: 1-85078-720-4

Cover design by fourninezero design.
Photography © Andrew Bessant, Nigel Cooke and Paul Gabb
Print Management by Adare Carwin
Printed in Great Britain by J.H. Haynes & Co., Sparkford

Contents

Introduction by the Chairman of the 2006 Convention

Hot, busy, fruitful. These are some of the the words that come to my mind as I look back on Keswick 2006.

It was certainly hot. The first two weeks were some of the hottest days in the UK for many years. Conventioners enjoyed long sunny days and warm evenings, crowned with magnificent sunsets.

It was busy. Numbers were good, seminar venues full to overflowing. The third week, in particular, saw a very healthy increase in attendance.

And fruitful. Certainly it was in my own life, as God spoke to me through his word again and again. Letters received since the Convention reveal the way God worked in many people's lives. A letter in the post this morning gave a remarkable testimony of God at work in the lives of a couple, culminating in their response to the call to involvement in mission.

Our thanks, then, not only to the preachers and those who led us in song, but to the willing army of hundreds of volunteers who make this Convention possible year after year.

To Ali Hull, who edits this volume, my thanks also. I trust it will serve as a great reminder to those who were present. If you're reading this and have never visited the Convention, I would love to have you join us.

On behalf of the Council,

Peter Maiden
September 2006

The Bible Readings

Gripes, grapes and grace in the wilderness

by Chris Wright

Chris Wright

Chris was ordained in the Church of England in 1977 and went on to teach in India for five years at Union Biblical Seminary. He is currently International Ministries Director of the Langham Partnership International. He loves preaching and teaching the Bible, which he does now mostly through the Langham Preaching seminars in different parts of the world and at All Souls Church, Langham Place, where he is a member of the staff team. He is married to Liz and they have four children.

Menus, management and the Spirit of God (1)
Numbers 10-11

Introduction

The theme of Keswick 2006 is The Church in the Power of the Spirit. I wonder if you heard of the story of the preacher who was expounding on the church as the body of Christ and he was warming to his theme: 'Some of us are like the mouth; God has given us gifts of speaking, and some of you are like ears with the gift of counselling and listening. Some, of course, are the hands and have practical discerning gifts.' Then he began to get a bit carried away: 'And some of you are the tonsils. We'd be better off without you! And some of you are like the appendix. We didn't know you were there at all until you started grumbling!'

Paul asked what the whole church would be like if it was just an ear or a hand. Moses probably thought that the Israelites, the whole body, had become a tonsil or an appendix, because they were a bunch of grumblers. Yet the power of the Holy Spirit is specifically there with these people, the Old Testament Israelites.

Looking back on this time, Nehemiah tells us in chapter 9:19-20 that 'By day the pillar of cloud did not cease to guide them on their path, nor the pillar of fire by night . . . You [God] gave your good Spirit to instruct them.' And Isaiah tells us in chapter 63:11-12 that the people of God

> recalled the days of old,
> the days of Moses and his people –
> where is he who brought them through the sea,
> with the shepherd of his flock?
> Where is he who set
> his Holy Spirit among them,
> who sent his glorious arm of power
> to be at Moses' right hand?

Here we have in the Old Testament a people who experienced the power of God, who lived with the leading and the power of the Holy Spirit and yet also faced huge problems. Let's not be tempted to be triumphalistic or naive as we look at this, or to imagine that just because the Spirit is with us, that everything in the garden is going to be rosy and all will be well.

Let me just survey the chapters we're going to look at very quickly. In chapter 11 we're going to be looking at the physical problems of food and meat and menus, and organisational problems that God had to sort out. Later we'll look at chapter 12, at jealousy between leaders and divisions right at the very heart of leadership. Then, in chapters 13-14, we will look at the problems of fear and unbelief in the people of God and outright rebellion for them. In chapter 16, we're going to look at the problem of people who are seeking status and ambition in God's kingdom and who completely misunderstand the problem of holiness and servanthood. Finally, we'll look at chapters 22-24, where we see a people who are threatened by external plotting, even if they don't know it; the story of Balaam and Balak. We'll see then how God turns it to a blessing and how they experience God's unseen protection against their enemies.

On the move again at last! (Num. 10:29-36)

There's been almost exactly a year since the Israelites left Egypt and arrived at Mount Sinai. Compare the date given in Numbers 10:11 with the date given in Exodus 19:1. And what a year it had been! There had been the miracles over Egypt as they left and the Passover; the great crossing at the Red Sea, the making of the covenant at Mount Sinai, all the spectacular experience that that had brought. There had been the terrible time when they had rebelled against God and almost been destroyed but had experienced God's forgiveness. Then they spent some months building the Tabernacle. But now it was time to move on. 'The LORD our God said to us at Horeb, "You have stayed long enough at this mountain"' (Deut. 1:6).

In 10:29, Moses turns to the family who had first welcomed him to Sinai: the family of Jethro, who was now his father-in-law. It's an interesting and slightly curious fact that the narrator of the whole section of the Sinai narrative begins and ends with the same people. It begins when the Israelites arrive at Sinai with Jethro welcoming them. Remember back to Exodus 18, where Jethro welcomes Moses, his son-in-law, to his part of the world. In Numbers 10, at the other end of the story as they are about to leave Sinai, Moses turns to Hobab, who was most probably Jethro's son and therefore Moses' brother-in-law, and invites him to accompany him on his journey. This family, Jethro and Hobab, were Midianites, part of the desert tribes. Later on they are called Kenites. Hobab initially declined but it seems that he eventually agreed because he turns up later in the story in the book of Judges (chapters 1 and 4) and we read about the Canaanite people of this particular community being among the Israelites later.

The question is: who was really leading the people at this point? God? Yes: we are told in verse 33 that the Ark of the Covenant, representing the very presence of God, was going before them as they moved, and the cloud of God's presence was to be seen by day and the pillar of fire by night. God was in charge.

What about Moses? Yes: in verse 35 Moses was the one who was appointed by God. He was summoned by God and had the authority to say when they were going to leave and where they would stop and camp. Surely God and Moses were in charge. So what about Hobab? In verse 31, Moses says to him 'You will be our eyes. You know where the water is, you know where the oasis is, you have the local expertise.' There is this very interesting combination here: Moses had God's authority, God's presence, God's guidance and yet he asks for Hobab's eyes. He is confident in God but doesn't despise human expertise and wisdom.

I think there's a lesson in that for us. It's a combination that we need to get in our Christian lives and as churches and Christian communities. One of the things that we are doing in the Langham Partnership at the moment is trying to establish regional councils around different parts of the world, in Africa, Asia and Latin America. When these small groups meet, this is a passage that I make them read with me. I say, 'Look, in the Langham Partnership, we believe that this is a ministry of God that God has established, but we need you as our eyes and ears in this part of the world. We want you to be our Hobabs to give us the wisdom and guidance and local knowledge that we can't possibly have.'

So the march of God's people begins. Here they are: led by God, with the presence of God's Spirit, led by Moses and a man with brilliant expertise, Hobab, and with the wonderful promises of good things that God has put ahead of them. Moses mentions twice to Hobab about the good things that God had promised to Israel. Surely, with such a list of advantages, these people are guaranteed success.

So chapter 11:1 is bit of a shock. 'The people complained about their hardships . . .' The word 'hardships' means evil. I'm sure that the narrator is quite deliberately contrasting the double use of 'good' in what Moses said to Hobab with this immediate use of 'evil' in the language and the attitude of the people. There is grumbling, rebellion, disobedience, division and judgement, and it's going to go on for chapter after chapter after chapter. A people, who are God's people in the power of the Spirit, are still a bunch of discontented grumbling rebels.

The first few verses of Numbers 11 are, I think, quite deliberately a short passage. Sometimes the Hebrew narrators like to do this. We start with a very short story of judgement; the complaints of the people of Taberah. The people complained, God got angry, fire comes out and there is judgement and burning: the people cry out, Moses intercedes and it dies down again. That's the pattern. That's what we're going to see repeatedly in these chapters. I've coined the phrase magic to express this, spelling it incorrectly as 'Majic': 'M' is for murmuring. 'A' is for anger; God's anger and sometimes Moses' anger. 'J' is for judgment and then 'I' is for intercession; Moses falls on his face again and again in these chapters; and finally 'C' is for containment. The problem is contained and the people move forward.

1. The menu crisis (11:4-6)

Verse 4: 'The rabble with them began to crave other food, and again the Israelites started wailing and said, "If only we had meat to eat! We remember the fish we ate in Egypt at no cost – also the cucumbers, melons, leeks, onions and garlic. But now we have lost our appetite; we never see anything but manna."'

What do you think the Israelites would have remembered the most about the years of slavery in Egypt? Just one year before this event they had been an oppressed, exploited minority, being beaten and put to slave labour in Egyptian agriculture and construction projects, doing all the dirty work that the Egyptians didn't want to do. What would they remember? The hard labour, the humiliation, the genocidal murder of the little boys? No. They remember *the fish*. It was very tasty and it was free. Talk about a selective memory! They'd been slaves for generations. So they reckon that a healthy diet in slavery is better than a normal diet in freedom. That's the perversity of what they are saying. They'd lost their chains and now they'd lost their appetite. They'd been having a miracle a day – manna, but it wasn't good enough and they found it boring.

Isn't this a very human narrative? So many of the problems among God's people involve the most ordinary things that you can think of. Cucumbers, melons, onions; food and their craving, their grumbling, their weeping and their wailing (that's what begins to happen): there is some sort of communal crying session and it precipitates another crisis . . .

2. The management crisis (11:10-15)

It became a massive community protest in verse 10: 'The LORD became exceedingly angry, and Moses was troubled.' That's actually a little weak. What it actually says is that it was evil in the eyes of Moses. The narrator is yet again contrasting the good things that were supposed to be happening at the end of chapter 10 with the evil that is happening now. Moses and God are quite rightly angry. Moses has told Hobab that things are going to be good, but now he sees that things have become terribly bad. And Moses falls into a crisis of his own leadership and management.

I'm going to read verses 11-15 in *The Message* version as I think that it captures better something of the bitterness and sarcasm in the language of Moses.

> Moses said to GOD, "Why are you treating me this way? What did I ever do to you to deserve this? Did I conceive them? Was I their mother? So why dump the responsibility of this people on me? Why tell me to carry them around like a nursing mother, carry them all the way to the land you promised to their ancestors? Where am I supposed to get meat for all these people who are whining to me, 'Give us meat; we want meat.' I can't do this by myself – it's too much, all these people. If this is how you intend to treat me, do me a favour and kill me. I've seen enough; I've had enough. Let me out of here."

It's ironic that Moses now accuses God of doing evil to him. It's the same word used here: 'God, why did you do evil to me?' He suggests that God should have taken his responsibility as a parent a little more seriously, and not dumped all the chores onto the nanny. He says 'Lord, I can't take it any more. If you really love me, shoot me now!' It's just as well that God doesn't always answer our prayers.

Moses Watch 1

At this point I want to look at one of the aspects of Moses's character that comes out at different points. What we see in this outburst is almost a complete collapse of his self-confidence as a leader. We can look at that in two ways. We can look at it positively, and say that at the very least Moses is not presented here as a James Bond figure. In all the great hero movies, it's amazing how quickly the hero comes up with a solution and always knows exactly what to do. Nor is Moses a management guru, expertly sitting down to diagnose the problem, coming up with creative ideas that will lead to solutions that everyone agrees to and then moves forward. Moses simply collapses. He hadn't always been like that. Remember Moses back in Exodus 2: there he showed instant action. He saw one Egyptian beating a Hebrew and he killed him: there are only two verses for that story. One verse has the problem and the other verse the solution. End of problem, thought Moses, and he ended up for forty years in the desert because of it.

Where will you find Moses now? Face down before the Lord in desperate inadequacy, desperate dependence. 'Lord, if there's going to be any answer to this problem, which I very much doubt, it's got to come from you.' There's an absence of self-sufficiency. But I think there's something more serious here. This crisis is causing Moses to doubt his own leadership, as well as causing him to doubt God himself and his very unrealistic demands. Pressures can arise even for the most gifted leaders.

Moses was a gifted leader. He has all the training, expertise and experience of forty years of government service under Pharaoh; he had every gift you could imagine. But at this point the pressures and the complaints are such that it becomes impossible. 'Where did I go wrong, if it's my fault? Where did you go wrong in expecting all of this anyway? I'm a failure, get me out of here!'

From verse 16 onwards, the narrator begins to show us how God solves this double crisis. He very cleverly reverses the order and records first of all what God said about the leadership (vs 16-17), then goes on to talk about the menu problem (vs 18-23), then comes back to the management problem (vs 24-30) interrupting the story about the meat and the quails, and finally comes back to the meat problem to tell us what happened to solve that (vs 31-34). The narrator wants to build up the suspense, for us to wonder what is going to happen next.

3. The management solution: (11:16-17, 24-30)

God says to Moses in verses 16

> Bring me seventy of Israel's elders who are known to you as leaders and officials among the people. Make them come to the Tent of Meeting, that they may stand there with you. I will come down and speak with you there, and I will take of the Spirit that is on you and put the Spirit on them. They will help you carry the burden of the people so that you will not have to carry it alone.

This is the first time that we hear that Moses is a man of God's Spirit; 'the Spirit that is on you.' What does that mean? It certainly doesn't mean that Moses had instant off-the-page solutions to every problem, nor did it give Moses some super status of his own. Remember that the man who God describes here in verse 17 as having 'the Spirit' is the man in verses 11-15 who wasn't able to cope. We might say, paradoxically, that the fact that he knew he had the Spirit of God reinforced a lack of self-sufficiency. Moses knew that only God could solve the problem, and yet he still felt alone, impotent and inadequate. So God said. 'I'll tell you what I'll do, I'll spread the Spirit around a bit for you. I'll put the Spirit on seventy more people so they can help you carry the load.'

Back in Exodus 18, the *administrative* load had already being shared and delegated on the advice of Jethro, so probably what this later event is talking about is more the sharing of spiritual leadership, of widening the circle of those that God had given gifts to, those who were able to speak the word of God to people and to administer pastoral wisdom. That's probably the difference between Exodus 18 and Numbers 11.

God said 'Get me seventy elders together' and Moses does it

> Moses went out and told the people what the LORD had said. He
> brought together seventy of their elders and made them stand around
> the Tent. Then the LORD came down in a cloud and spoke with him,
> and he took of the Spirit that was on him and put the Spirit on the
> seventy elders. When the Spirit rested on them, they prophesied, but
> they did not do so again (Num. 11:24-25).

Moses Watch 2

We see at this point in the story that not only was Moses completely
lacking in self-sufficiency, he was also perfectly willing to share the
Spirit. He was willing to accept the gifts of the Spirit to and in other
people, and that is a sign of Moses' own spiritual maturity. Moses says,
'That's fine, God: I need it.' That's exactly what happens in verses 24–
25: the elders come together and are there before the watching
people. They need some mark of authentication, that they are now
going to exercise a spiritual leadership, approved and inspired by God
alongside Moses. They're not appointed by some election among the
people, they're summoned here by God's representative and God
authenticates them by letting them prophesy, which probably means
that they speak some kind of word from God.

Then in verse 26, all the shared leadership goes bottom up too.
Two men, whose names were Eldad and Medad, had remained in the
camp. They were listed or registered among the elders but they
hadn't gone out to the tent. Yet the Spirit also rested on them and
they prophesied inside the camp. So here we have an outburst of
unscrip-ted, unsupervised charismatic activity. Outside the control of
Moses, these people are prophesying.

We don't know why Eldad and Medad didn't come to the tent, but
they're not blamed for it. They were late but God fills them also with
the Spirit and they manifest the authentic prophesying words of God.
God is merciful; he even looks after the latecomers. Then in verse 28,
Joshua, son of Nun, Moses' assistant, speaks up and says 'My Lord, stop
them.' Objections come from the number 2 leader. I wonder why.
Perhaps he was concerned this was a breach of good order, perhaps he

thought it was bad manners, perhaps he was afraid of a loss of control, or he thought it was an implied insult to Moses. And this upset him more than Moses.

I'm sure that you have observed the fact that when people are put on pedestals, in some positions of senior leadership, you often find a bunch of acolytes around who draw their own authority and status from being servants of the servants of God. Anything that threatens the leader's authority also threatens theirs. Quite possibly what's going on here is that Joshua sees the threat to Moses' authority and wonders how it's going to affect him.

I wonder if this is something that happens too in the gospels. In Luke 9, when the disciples discovered that there was someone out there who was casting out demons in the name of Jesus, they said, 'Lord, we tried to stop him.' Jesus replied in verse 50, 'Whoever is not against you is for you.' Jesus had the same relaxed attitude to what is going on as Moses does here. In verse 29 we have Moses' reply, which is wonderful. You don't get facial expressions in the Scriptures but I wish we did. 'Are you jealous for my sake?' he asks, as if to say, 'It's not a problem to me, so what are you jealous about?' It's a wonderful answer.

Moses Watch 3

We see in Moses a complete absence of personal jealousy. He had no desire for office, status or prestige. He hadn't even asked for this job, and had done everything he could to get out of it. If God wanted to share his gifts around, it was no problem for Moses. In fact, he says that he wishes all of God's people were prophets. Perhaps he thought that if they were all prophets, he wouldn't have to be the one sorting out everyone else's problems! Perhaps it was simply that Moses had a deep security in his relationship with God. He had no need to prove anything and that in itself is a mark of great spiritual maturity.

Our reactions in church and the Christian world, especially when things are unexpected and not quite what we want, can very easily be like Joshua's. 'Stop them; we can't have that going on.' Or our reaction can be like that of Moses. Moses is behaving here a bit like Barnabas, when he saw all the activity in a church outside Jerusalem.

It must have been very different from his Jewish upbringing, but we read in Acts that 'when Barnabas saw the grace of God, he was glad.'

4. The menu solution (11:18-23, 31-35)

In verses 18-20 we read God's reaction to the people. God perceives much more in what the people are whining about than simply boredom with manna

> Tell the people 'Consecrate yourselves in preparation for tomorrow, when you will eat meat. The LORD heard you when you wailed, "If only we had meat to eat! We were better off in Egypt!" Now the LORD will give you meat, and you will eat it. You will not eat it for just one day, or two days, or five, ten or twenty days, but for a whole month – until it comes out of your nostrils and you loathe it – because you have rejected the LORD, who is among you.'

What happens here, as God sees it, is that God's people are turning away from the whole project of salvation. These people are seriously losing the plot. The Israelites had been crying out in the slavery crisis in Exodus and now they are saying 'We were better off in Egypt.' They had the living God among them, but now they had rejected him. 'So' says God, 'you want meat, I'll give you meat until you're sick of it.'

Let me read a paraphrase of verses 21 and 22 for Moses' response. 'I'm standing here surrounded by six thousand men on foot and you say I'll give you meat for a month. So where's it all coming from, then? Even if all the flocks and heads were butchered, would that be enough? Even if all the fish in the sea were caught, would that be enough?'

It's really quite sarcastic. There's a wonderful little play on words, even in the midst of all that, in between verses 20 and 21. In verse 20, God says 'I am the LORD who is *among* you': in verse 21, Moses says, 'I am here *among* these people.' God says that 'The people I am *among* have rejected me' and Moses says 'The people I am *among* just want meat.' God's answer in verse 23 is equally cryptic, and again the narrator builds up our suspense: 'The LORD answered Moses, "Is the

LORD's arm too short? You will now see whether or not what I say will come true for you.'"

I love the way in which Raymond Brown comments on this particular point and the comparison he makes: 'You see the menu that the people were craving was fish and vegetables; the menu that Moses was imagining when he talked about slaughtering the herd was beef and lamb and fish. But the menu that God had in mind was poultry. And it was on its way already!'[1]

So we come to meat at the end of the story, but it is meat with judgement (vs 31-34)

> Now a wind went out from the LORD and drove quail in from the sea. It brought them down all around the camp to about three feet above the ground, as far as a day's walk in any direction. All that day and night and all the next day the people went out and gathered quail.

These people again show how short their memory was because they should have remembered that almost exactly a year ago God had enabled them to benefit from the annual spring migration of millions of birds that moved northwards from Africa across Palestine and Lebanon and on into the north. But whereas last time the quails were a gift of God that brought a blessing, this time they come as a gift that brings judgement.

The writer tells us in verse 31 'a wind went out from the LORD.' In Hebrew that's the word *ruah* which is exactly the word that is translated otherwise as Spirit. The Spirit of God solved the management crisis in the middle of the chapter, and now the *ruah*, the wind of God, solved the meat crisis that brings so much meat in on the wind that the people are able to net it and everyone had buckets full. But then it leads to serious illness, as we read in verse 33: 'But while the meat was still between their teeth . . . the anger of the LORD burned against the people, and he struck them with a severe plague.'

What does this mean? It probably means that before the actual supply of birds was finished, it went bad. The plague that is described is quite possibly food poisoning. They didn't let it dry out properly, they didn't salt it properly, as they still do in those parts of the world where birds are captured. Either that or it's the first recorded case of bird flu! But it results in more graves in the wilderness. The place, in English, was called 'Graves of craving.' The people craved meat and it leads to their punishment and suffering.

That's the story of this chapter. I hope that we have learned three things in conclusion. The first is that, as in physical disease, the presenting symptoms of a problem may well hide more serious dangerous disorders. In church, complaints about simple things like food and rotas and the use of money can actually hide a deeper discontent and a deeper failure, especially the failure to understand the deeper plan and purpose of God for us as a church. Sometimes our behaviour can be so thoughtless and faithless and we can be so short in our memories. In spite of all the good things that God has built into the past, and all the good things that he has for the future, we effectively put God's purposes in rewind. We need to be careful about what lies beneath when there is a culture of complaints and protest in any Christian community.

The second thing is that Spirit-filled leadership does not mean spiritual superheroes who are omni-competent. What we find here is the paradox that the evidence of the presence of the Spirit of God in the life of Moses is the absence of the things that the world usually links to strong leadership: self-sufficiency, status, ambition and control. In that, he proves that he was being led by the Spirit of God.

Thirdly, we see by looking at Moses that the Spirit is for sharing. Even though God does raise up remarkable individuals within his community of people, of all ages, it is still intended by God that it is a shared leadership, exercised alongside the gift of others. The New Testament clearly endorses this: the Spirit of God distributed his gifts not just for the one man at the top but to be shared. These things were written for our learning, so may the Holy Spirit help us to learn what is here. Amen.

Endnote:

[1] Raymond Brown, *The Message of Numbers* (IVP: BST series, Nottingham, 2002), p96.

Humility, authority and the approval of God (2)
Numbers 12

Introduction

In the very last chapter of Deuteronomy, Deuteronomy 34, we read that 'no prophet has risen in Israel like Moses, whom the LORD knew face to face, who did all those miraculous signs and wonders the LORD sent him to do in Egypt . . . For no one has ever shown the mighty power or performed the awesome deeds that Moses did in the sight of all Israel' (vs 10-12).

Yet according to Numbers 12:3, Moses was a very humble man, more humble than anyone else on the face of the world. It really is a remarkable paradox when you put those two Scriptures together. Moses was the great deliverer, the great law-giver; he was undoubtedly one of the greatest leaders that mankind has ever known. Yet we are told here that he was the most humble man on the planet. So this story in Numbers 12 is very subtle, showing this paradox between authority in this God-approved, Spirit-filled leader, the one who was speaking on behalf on God, and the man who was humble and barely speaks a word in this chapter. And even when he does speak, it's not in his own defence. What we are going to see here is a subtle combination of authority and humility, stretched and tested, and how God affirmed his approval and his authority for Moses, through whom his revelation comes.

1. The leadership conflict around Moses (12:1–3)

'Miriam and Aaron began to talk against Moses because of his Cushite wife, for he had married a Cushite. "Has the LORD spoken only through Moses?" they asked. "Hasn't he also spoken through us?" And the LORD heard this.' This summarises a very complex situation that seems a little puzzling. We can't always see the precise connection between what they are complaining about and what they actually say, so the narrative answers a whole series of issues that are being wrapped up in this ugly quarrel. There are at least five aspects in the leadership conflict that we can see.

A family issue

Moses was the kid brother. He was an eighty-year-old kid brother, but he was still the kid brother. I'm the youngest of four and my older sister still thinks of me as her kid brother. Once a kid brother, always a kid brother; that's the situation here. Aaron was the oldest in the family in the genealogy in Exodus 6:20. Miriam was certainly Moses' older sister because she was a little girl when he was only a baby. And these two become peeved and jealous that Moses is still getting all this limelight, after all these years. You can imagine Aaron saying, 'Who did all that hard talking to Pharaoh when Moses told God that he couldn't speak up and God had to make me his spokesperson? Did I get the credit? No.' And you can imagine Miriam saying, 'Yeah, and who helped Pharaoh's daughter fetch Moses out of the Nile when he was about to drown, the little cry-baby?'

As you read the story, you realise that Aaron had had a rough ride. He gets the blame, not entirely wrongly, for the great apostasy of the Golden Calf in Exodus 32, when his brother was up the mountain for a month and no one knew what had happened to him. Shortly after this, Aaron had lost two of his four sons in Leviticus 10. Miriam is almost unheard of in the narrative after she leads the singing after the

Exodus. So there is this sibling rivalry; jealousy between family members called into leadership amongst God's people.

This can still be a very serious problem in God's people and the churches. Many of us know situations where a single family has all been in leadership together in a church, organisation or mission, and it's not always the case that things are harmonious amongst them. Psalm 133 tells us how good it is when brothers dwell together in unity, and the psalmist could well have added a Hebrew parallelism on how rare and unusual it is too.

A leadership issue

Moses, Aaron and Miriam represent the senior leadership of Israel at this time in their history, and all of them were God-appointed to the roles that they were playing. Micah 6:4 tells us 'I brought you up out of Egypt and redeemed you from the land of slavery. I sent Moses to lead you, also Aaron and Miriam.' They were God-appointed.

Aaron was a high priest, the head of the whole priesthood in Israel, who would call on him. He was the embodiment of the holiness of God and he represented too the ideal sanctuary of Israel and the holy people of God. Miriam was a prophet, like her brother Moses. You don't hear much of her but we read in Exodus 15 that she was apparently the Spirit-filled leader of the women in the community, who led the singing and praise of God. So we have an alliance of priest and prophet conspiring together against Moses as God's appointed leader, questioning his role and unique status as mediator between God and his people. This is a potentially catastrophic challenge to the whole leadership of God's people. These three people were all appointed by God and yet they fell out in this nasty conflict.

We need to be realistic about our leaders, even our leaders who are filled with the Spirit. They are still humans and sinners as well as saints. Serious conflict can arise between leaders and endanger the whole work of God.

An ethnic issue

In verse 1 we read that Miriam and Aaron complained about Moses' wife, who was a Cushite. This ethnic identity is mentioned twice in the same verse, as if we need to know it twice. But there is some mystery about this woman: who was she? Was this another way of referring to Zipporah, who was the daughter of Jethro? Some scholars think that, but I think most certainly not. Zipporah was a Midianite, and this woman is called a Cushite. Midian and Cush are two different places. So was this woman a second wife? Almost certainly yes. In that case, we have to ask was Zipporah dead? I think probably not. Of course we cannot be ultimately sure because the narrative doesn't tell us, but we are told in Exodus 18 that Jethro had only just brought Zipporah back to meet with Moses when he had come out of all the struggles in Egypt and returned to Sinai. She had lived with her father whilst Moses was in Egypt and they had only just been reunited a few months earlier. So Moses had married two people, and both of them were foreign.

The more important question is: what was she, this Cushite wife? She was a black African. The land of Cush was an important, powerful kingdom just to the south of biblical Egypt, what we would now call southern Egypt, or upper Nile Egypt or part of northern Sudan. It was actually a strongly influential kingdom through the whole of the Old Testament period. It played an important role in Egyptian politics and the international politics of the Middle East. There are in fact over fifty references to Cush and Cushites in the Old Testament. It's a little confusing because sometimes the word is translated as Ethiopia and the biblical Ethiopia was not territorially the same as modern Ethiopia. The common biblical name is Cush and the Cushites were black Africans. Some of them reigned over Egypt at one time: during that time the Pharaohs were Cushites. Very probably Cushites, black Africans, were among the mixed multitudes that came out of Egypt along with the Israelites.

The third question we have to ask is: why did Miriam and Aaron object to this marriage? We can only guess, but we can at least seek to give a provisional answer to the question. Was it because she was black? The emphasis was on the fact that she was a Cushite, and we know that the Cushites were proverbial for their black skin. That's why Jeremiah uses them as an example of something that cannot be changed: 'Can a Cushite change his skin or a leopard change his spots?'

Or was it simply because she was foreign? It's important to say that, at this point, Moses has not actually broken the law of God. Some people say he shouldn't have married a foreigner because the Israelites were prohibited from marrying foreigners. Well, only *some* foreigners. Deuteronomy 7 was going to tell the Israelites that they must not marry *Canaanite* women. That was not for ethnic reasons but for religious reasons: they would draw them away into the worship of other gods. This woman was a Cushite, not a Canaanite.

Or was it because she was a second wife and so it was an unfair treatment of Zipporah? We can't be sure, but whatever it was that Miriam and Aaron objected to in Moses' marriage, it was not a problem for God. *God* does not condemn Moses for this inter-ethnic marriage. Nevertheless, the ethnic issue itself seems to be a part of this conflict within the family and leadership of God's people. Ethnic prejudice and racial hatred were infecting and poisoning the people of God, just as they can today.

We're not just talking here about white racism: racism and ethnic prejudice can be found all through the world and in all different cultures – it can be there among Chinese and Korean Christians; you can go to India and find a church that is shredded by all kinds of suspicions and rivalry between people of different regional and language backgrounds. You go to Africa and you find churches riddled with tribalism and splits and so on. This is a reality that we still face in the world today.

A spiritual issue

This comes in verse 2. It's difficult to see the precise connection between verses 1 and 2, but it seems that all this fuss about the wife of Moses actually concealed a deeper criticism and complaint that goes to the heart of the issue. Moses was the one through whom God was revealing his will, law and word, and Miriam and Aaron are complaining about that.

At this point, even among the prophets that God had raised up, and would raise up, Moses was still unique. We need to recognise that in terms of biblical history and salvation, at this stage of the biblical revelation, Moses occupied a unique position. It was not because he claimed or wanted it but because God had chosen him and put him there. It is this that Miriam and Aaron question in their two questions in verse 2.

These questions point in two different directions. The first question is: 'Has the LORD spoken only through Moses?' They are questioning Moses' uniqueness in his relationship with God, the one who was the unique communicator of God's revelation. They ask 'Is that what we are meant to accept?' And the second question is: 'Hasn't he also spoken through us?' That is questioning Moses' uniqueness in relation to the rest of Moses' leadership team.

'Don't we all have important gifts? I'm a prophet' says Miriam. 'What's so special about Moses?' It's the classic 'Who does he think he is?' that is going on here. It's a very familiar tactic among the discontented and the disaffected and insinuates an arrogance about Moses that the narrator is going to tell us is not there. It accuses him of a monopoly that he didn't want; it implies that Moses was hogging all the gifts and status, when in fact that was the opposite to what he wanted, as we're told in chapter 11.

And so Aaron and Miriam protest. Both of them had God-given gifts and responsibilities of their own. This is a case of spiritual jealousy and discontent and an attack on a brother. It may have looked like a family feud but there was a profoundly spiritual issue attached.

A character issue

There is a contrast between the way Aaron and Miriam are behaving and the way Moses reacts. We read that Miriam and Aaron began to talk against Moses. We want to ask where and to whom. To each other? To other people? To other family members? And they asked whom? Themselves? Anyone who would listen? The rest of the Levites? There's a campaign going on, a subtle subversive undermining of Moses. But what does Moses say in response? Nothing. And you get the feeling that the narrator gets embarrassed by his silence. The narrator says that the Lord heard what they were saying but Moses said nothing, and the reason was that Moses was the most humble man on earth. Moses was not a character who got into a dog fight of attack, defence and counter-attack. There was a dignified silence.

One of the things that I've learnt in my limited experience of Christian leadership is that self-defence is rarely, if ever, the right response to being attacked, accused or misinterpreted. The more you try and defend yourself, the more you dig yourself into the hole, the more you make the accusations sounds as if they are true. Humility is the very essence of a Christian leader amongst God's people. One commentator says 'Moses' uniqueness was neither self-claimed nor self-defended; his uniqueness lay not in asserting his own claims, but in the humility that led him not to.'

But God's own authority and own revelation were bound up with Moses' at this point, so if Moses wasn't going to defend himself, God certainly was.

Before we move on, let's summarise the seriousness of what is happening here. We have a people who are being led by God and by people who are filled with God's Spirit; people who are appointed and equipped for all aspects of Christian leadership. And yet there is family quarrelling and jealousy, there are strong suspicions of ethnic prejudice and a criticism of a brother's marriage, there are accusations of monopoly and a campaign of undermining intended to bring a brother down. Do you recognise any of that? Isn't that what goes on, sometimes, in some of our churches? The power and presence of God's Spirit doesn't automatically mean the end of all such problems caused by our humanity and fallenness, even at the highest level.

2. God's confidence in Moses (12:4-9)

God deals with the quarrel by directly confronting the participants and by calling them together into his presence. We all know those words of Jesus that we hope to hear ourselves, 'Well done, good and faithful servant.' Most of us expect to die before we hear them. What happens here is that Moses hears them at this precise point of accusation.

A faithful servant in God's house

We already know that Moses was humble. But now God adds some other things – at least three things. The first is that Moses was a faithful servant: 'my servant Moses; he is faithful in all my house' (v7). That in itself is a term of high honour combined with humble status. He's my servant, says the Lord. This title of 'my servant' is given to very few people in the Old Testament. God says this about Caleb, for example, in Numbers 14; it's said about David quite regularly, but it's a rare term of honour, speaking about someone who was going to do the will and purpose of God. The fact that Moses is God's servant means that he has access to the whole of his estate. God is saying, 'All of my affairs are entrusted into his hands.' God is saying that he has exercised trust in Moses; he trusted him to confront Pharaoh and to stand firm in all the pressures of the plagues. He trusted Moses to lead this people, he trusted Moses to reveal his law and his name, as Yahweh the God of Israel. And God says 'my servant Moses has not been a disappointment to me. He has been faithful in every department of my house.' It doesn't mean that he didn't make any mistakes, but God is saying that Moses is a trustworthy house manager.

The unique receiver of God's revelation

God distinguished between ordinary everyday prophets, to whom he gives messages and dreams, and Moses. With Moses, it's different, he says: 'With him I speak face to face.' Literally, if we look at verse 8, that's mouth to mouth. God says that 'Moses speaks what I say.' There is a direct correlation between the word of Moses and the word of God. God's law and truth and self-revelation at this point in biblical history are coming through this man of God. That is part of the reason for the scriptural authority of Moses. Not only was Moses God's servant, he was also God's friend. There is this unique intimacy that Moses has with God.

Listen to Exodus 33:11-13

> The LORD would speak to Moses face to face, as a man speaks with his friend . . . Moses said to the LORD, "You have been telling me, 'Lead these people,' but you have not let me know whom you will send with me. You have said, 'I know you by name and you have found favour with me.' If you are pleased with me, teach me your ways so I may know you . . ."

Moses wanted to know God as a friend, and God honoured that request. So in Numbers 12:8, God says that Moses 'saw the form' of the Lord. It doesn't mean that Moses saw God as he was, but that Moses clearly saw some visible experience of the presence of God. Exodus 24, the story of the making of the Covenant, tells of some people who saw God. They had a one-off visible experience of the presence of God. The rest of the people, we are told in Deuteronomy 4:12,15, 'saw no form', there was only a voice on the day that the Lord spoke through the fire. Moses had a unique experience of the presence of God, so much so that when he went out of the presence of God, his face was shining in such a way that the people were afraid of him. God affirms his approval of his chosen leader Moses – not because of his great power or resourcefulness or managerial skills – but because he was a humble man, a faithful servant, a unique communicator and a true friend of God.

Moses claimed none of these things for himself; these are the things that God says about Moses. So God says to Aaron and Miriam, 'How dare you try and undermine this man? You're in danger of arguing against God.'

A clear anticipation of God's Son

Before we move on to see God's final act of vindication and the punishment that he inflicted on Miriam and Aaron, let's see the third aspect of what God says, that is not said directly here in the text but is picked up in the New Testament. We see here a clear anticipation of God's Son. In all of these ways, Moses is a portrait of the Lord Jesus Christ.

Humility

Moses was a humble man; so was Jesus. That's how he's assessed in Isaiah 53:2-3: 'He had no beauty or majesty to attract us to him, nothing in his appearance that we should desire him. He was despised and rejected by men, a man of sorrows, and familiar with suffering.' Jesus said 'Whoever wants to be great must be your servant, for even the Son of Man did not come to be served but to serve and to give his life as a ransom for many.'

Faithfulness

But also he was God's faithful Servant and Son. The writer of the book of Hebrews picks up on this language of Moses and applies it to Jesus in Hebrews 3:6: 'Christ was faithful as a son over God's house.' In the verse before he says, 'Moses was faithful as a servant in all God's house, testifying to what would be said in the future.' Jesus knew that he was coming from the Father and going to the Father, he was secure in his own Sonship, and so he was able to take the status of a servant and act humbly.

The unique revelation of God

We read in Hebrews 1:1-2, 'God spoke to our forefathers through the prophets at many times and in various ways, but in these last days he has spoken to us by his Son.' Whereas Moses saw the form of God, Jesus was in the form of God, as Paul puts it in Philippians 2

> Christ Jesus:
> Who, being in very nature God,
> did not consider equality with God something to be grasped,
> but made himself nothing,
> taking the very nature of a servant,
> being made in human likeness.
> And being found in appearance as a man,
> he humbled himself
> and became obedient to death –
> even death on a cross!

God's words about Moses, although historically true about him, were prophetically true about Jesus, who also bears the mark of God's approval. And this is the reason that God acts to defend the man who would not defend himself.

We read in verse 10 that Miriam is afflicted with a skin disease, not leprosy in its modern form but probably some form of flaking skin disorder which is described as being like snow. It may be that the narrator is seeing here some kind of poetic justice, that Miriam is afflicted with a disease that turns her white when she has accused Moses for taking a wife who was black. It is possible, as many commentators have suggested. But since the word 'white' is not mentioned, it simply says 'like snow,' it may simply mean a skin condition where the skin was flaking and falling off like snow, which would make more sense.

Aaron is horrified; in that culture the shame on his sister was also a shame on him. The irony is that Aaron had complained that Moses was usurping the full right to pray and speak to God, but now Aaron doesn't feel it right to go straight into the presence of God, high priest though he was, and turns to Moses. And here for the first time Moses speaks – the only time he speaks in this chapter. And when he speaks he speaks in prayer, to pray for his sister: 'O God, please heal her!' (v13). This is a mark of the likeness of Christ who told us that we should love those who persecute us, and who said 'Father, forgive them for they do not know what they are doing.' Moses prays 'O God, please heal her!' And God does so, after a period of time – a week of disgrace in which the lesson will be learnt by Miriam and the whole community. They will all wait for the problem to clear up and then they move forward with the problem solved.

Raymond Brown in his commentary puts it like this: 'Moses learnt the importance of silence and let the LORD do the talking . . . Aaron learnt the value of prayer' – though he was a high priest, he had to learn the power of the prayer of others (his own brother): 'Miriam learnt the generosity of grace' because eventually she was pardoned, cleansed, healed and restored, and 'the people learnt the seriousness of sin' although we have to say that they didn't learn it very well.

What about us? What do we learn? It depends whether we identify ourselves with Aaron and Miriam or Moses. Does the Holy Spirit say to us that we are behaving like Moses or Aaron in this story? Could it be that some of us are critical, undermining and jealous, guilty of discontent? If so, let's repent of our ways.

Or it may be we need to learn the lesson of Moses' leadership, if God has put us in leadership; the lesson that spiritual authority and personal humility are not incompatible but integral to each other; that the one is part of the other. It is because Moses was a humble man that God exalted and lifted him up. 'The one who is the greatest in the kingdom of God is the one who is least and the servant of all' as I quoted earlier from the words of Jesus Christ. May that be our ambition, for God's Name's sake and glory. Amen.

Espionage, rebellion and the patience of God (3)

Numbers 13

Introduction

Sometimes the Bible provides sermons on its own texts, and that's what we get in Deuteronomy 1. In chapters 1-3, Moses remembers what happened in the book of Numbers and preaches to the next generation of Israelites on the basis of this. Have this in mind as we turn to Numbers 13-14.

This is the great rebellion that happened in Kadesh. It was, in many ways, the most awful catastrophe in Israel's history up to this point. This rebellion became legendary in the Old Testament and is referred to several times in the New Testament as the classic instance of the rebellion of God's people against him, and of God's anger, which led to a whole generation being lost in the wilderness. This resulted in a setback, delaying God's plan for forty years. It is, in many ways, similar to the great apostasy of the Golden Calf that happened at Mount Sinai in Exodus 33-34.

I want us to look at three aspects of it: firstly at the spies' report and the people's rebellion, and some of the ingredients of the rebellion. Secondly, we will look at God's anger and Moses' appeal, and at Moses as a model of intercession; four things in his intercession will strike us. Finally, we will look at God's punishment but also his patience.

1. The spies' report and the people's rebellion (13:1 – 14:10)

The Israelites arrive at the very southern edges of the land of promise, the oasis that was there at Kadesh, and they decide to send out spies into the land (Num. 13:1-2). The spies come back and the report that they give is at first very positive (v26): 'They came back to Moses and Aaron and the whole Israelite community . . . There they reported to them and to the whole assembly and they showed them the fruit of the land.' They had brought back a whole big bunch of grapes as evidence of the fruitfulness of the land, and they gave this account to Moses: 'We went into the land to which you sent us, and it does flow with milk and honey!'

But then something happens. In verse 28 the spies' report very suddenly shifts into a grossly exaggerated negative account

> 'But the people who live there are powerful, and the cities are fortified and very large. We even saw descendants of Anak there . . . the Hittites, Jebusites and Amorites live in the hill country; and the Canaanites live near the sea and along the Jordan.' Then Caleb silenced the people before Moses and said, 'We should go up and take possession of the land, for we can certainly do it.'

Caleb says 'We can' and then in verse 30 one of the other ten spies says 'Sorry, but we can't.' There is a clash of reports. Then in verses 32-33, the rest of the spies spread negativity among the people. 'We can't attack the people, we seemed like grasshoppers in our own eyes.' As Raymond Brown puts it, 'They magnified the problem and then minimised the resources that they had' and the spies' report leads to the people's rebellion. In chapter 14 we read, 'That night all the people of the community raised their voices and wept aloud. All the Israelites grumbled against Moses and Aaron and the whole assembly said to them, "If only we had died in Egypt! Or in this desert!"' The narrator very clearly describes this very serious rebellion, involving the whole people.

What are the factors involved? What was causing the Israelites to take this attitude? This is where the commentary that we have in Deuteronomy 1:9-46 is helpful, because Moses, in his memory, isolates three factors in particular.

Rebellion against God's plans

He says 'But you were unwilling to go up; you rebelled against the command of the LORD your God. You grumbled in your tents and said, "The LORD hates us; so he brought us out of Egypt to deliver us into the hands of the Amorites to destroy us"' (vs 26-27).

There is this grumbling rebellion against God and a rejection of God's plans, the whole purpose of the redemption. The Israelites had been brought out of Egypt and they wanted to go back. Even worse than that, they attributed false motives to God. They said 'He only brought us out of slavery because he wanted to kill us here.' And then they said 'The Lord *hates* us,' (Deut. 1:27 emphasis added). That's incredible. What they had just experienced was the biggest demonstration of the love and faithfulness of God in the entire Bible, apart from in the cross: the story of the Exodus. It's the Old Testament story of God's redemption, faithfulness, love and power. God has poured his love on these people and they have turned around and said, 'Do you know what? God hates us.'

Sometimes people get very perverse in times of fear and depression. And so the people say (vs 2-3) 'We'd rather be dead. We'd rather go back to slavery.' What is God's response? God says 'How long will these people treat me with contempt, and how long will they refuse to believe in me?' It's very strong language. It's the kind of language that is used about David's adultery with Bathsheba. There again, we read through Nathan, David was treating the Lord with arrogant contempt, despising him. It's also talked about by Isaiah; he says that the Israelites are like a son who should honour his father, or an ox who should honour his owner. 'My people' says God 'are treating me with contempt.'

This rebellion in the wilderness is not just a rejection of Moses or the leadership, it is a rejection of God himself. Joshua points out, in chapter 14:8-9, that these people have an option. They can either please God and have God be pleased with them, through courage, obedience and faith or they can oppose and stand against God and be afraid of those whom God has already defeated. Joshua tries to persuade them to please God but they are in a state of grumbling rebellion.

Fear and an inferiority complex

The second thing that Moses pinpoints both here and in Deuteronomy 1 is fear and an inferiority complex. In Deuteronomy 1:28-29, he is retelling the story to the Israelites and reminding them how they reacted when they said 'Our brothers have made us lose heart. They say, "The people are stronger and taller than we are; the cities are large, with walls up to the sky. We even saw the Anakites there." Then I said to you, "Do not be terrified; do not be afraid of them."'

Obviously the Israelites *had* been afraid. The ten spies were sowing an inferiority complex amongst the people. 'We felt like grasshoppers, they were great big giants.' There is this graphic contrast. Even the land, they say in verse 32, 'devours its people . . .' But where did they get that from? This is a gross exaggeration, but it led to fear.

It is possible, even as a Christian, to cringe and feel 'I'm too small, I don't have any strength, I'm inferior.' Here were people who were defeated before they even got there. I remember when I was a little boy, learning to play rugby in Belfast. You'd go out on to the field and there were great big fellows in the opposing team, and somehow, when the teacher said to encourage us, 'The bigger they are, the harder they fall,' it didn't do very much to comfort you. 'The bigger they are, the harder they hurt' is usually what happened.

Unbelief in spite of the evidence

Numbers 14:11: 'The LORD said to Moses, "How long will these people treat me with contempt? How long will they refuse to believe in me, in spite of all the miraculous signs I have performed among them?"' Moses remembers these words and he says them directly to the Israelites. In Deuteronomy 1:31-33 he says 'You saw how the LORD your God carried you . . . until you reached this place. In spite of this, you did not trust in the LORD your God, who went ahead of you on your journey, in fire by night and in a cloud by day.' So they end up here, in sheer frustrating unbelief.

It's the same thing that vexed Jesus all through his ministry. Remember when Jesus was unable to do any good work because of the unbelief among the people. 'O ye of little faith' he once said to his disciples. And of course unbelief can afflict us at any point, even as mature Christian believers, when we're confronted with a future that seems uncertain or when God calls us into some new path of obedience. It's one thing to sing and celebrate all that God has done in the past, but am I going to be quite sure that 'all I will need your hand will provide?' Unbelief can weave into our heart and lead to disobedience.

It's a terrible moment, a mass rebellion. They refuse to go any further. They want to go back, and in verse 10 they even threaten to lynch Moses and Joshua. This is so serious that it echoes on through the Bible. In Psalm 106 we read

> Then they despised the pleasant land;
> they did not believe his promise.
> They grumbled in their tents
> and did not obey the LORD.
> So he swore to them with uplifted hand
> that he would make them fall in the desert,
> make their descendants fall among the nations
> and scatter them throughout the lands (vs 24-27).

In the New Testament, Paul mentions this rebellion in 1 Corinthians 10 and so does the writer of Hebrews, in chapter 3:16-19

> Who were they who heard and rebelled? Were they not all those Moses led out of Egypt? And with whom was he angry for forty years? Was it not with those who sinned, whose bodies fell in the desert? And

to whom did God swear that they would never enter his rest if not to those who disobeyed? So we see that they were not able to enter, because of their unbelief.

2. God's anger and Moses' appeal (14:11-19)

Moses recalls God's reaction very clearly in Deuteronomy 1:35. He says 'When the LORD heard what you said, he was angry and solemnly swore, "Not a man of this evil generation shall see the good land."' In Numbers 14, God puts his finger exactly on the things that we have been mentioning, their rejection of him and their unbelief, and as result of this he threatens complete destruction. God says in Numbers 14:12, 'I will strike them down with a plague and destroy them, but I will make you into a nation greater and stronger than they.' God is saying to Moses 'We're going to wipe this lot out. The whole lot of them, we're going to destroy in an instant, and then I'll start all over again. We'll forget about the children of Israel and we'll start to talk about the children of Moses.' That's what God is saying, effectively.

This is a threat and suggestion that God had actually made before in Exodus 32:10, as Moses came down from Mount Sinai during the incident with the Golden Calf: 'Get out of my way, Moses, that I might destroy these people and start again with you.' Once again, Moses repudiates the very idea and once again we find Moses stepping into the breach and standing between the people and the wrath of God, interceding for them and appealing to God to hold back his anger and bear their sin.

God's reputation

In this great prayer, the first thing that Moses appeals to is God's reputation, in verses 13-16. Yahweh, the God of Israel, was already making a name for himself around the region. When they had come out of Egypt after crossing the sea, Moses says in Exodus 15:14-15: 'The Philistines are trembling in their boots, so are the Canaanites and the Amorites. All these people have seen this and they are scared.' They know what this Yahweh God can do and they are scared. They know that his presence is in the midst of this people. 'So if you turn round and kill them, God, how do you think they will feel about you? What conclusion will they draw? Either they will think that you are incompetent as God or that you are malicious. They will think you brought the Israelites out of Egypt, planned a future for them but your plan collapsed, or brought them out to raise their hopes and then dash them. Is this what you want people to be saying about you?'

Moses' concern here is the name of the Lord in the midst of the nations. That is the motivation both for prayer and mission. That is what dominates the prophets such as Ezekiel, who says eighty times, 'Then you will know' . . . 'Then they will know' . . . 'Then the nations will know who God is because of what he does.' Moses is concerned about the name and reputation of God.

God's character

Verses 17–19

> Now may the Lord's strength be displayed, just as you have declared: "The LORD is slow to anger, abounding in love and forgiving sin and rebellion. Yet he does not leave the guilty unpunished; he punishes the children for the sin of the fathers to the third and fourth generation." In accordance with your great love, forgive the sin of these people, just as you have pardoned them from the time they left Egypt until now.

In Exodus, after that awful incident of the Golden Calf, Moses asked to see God's glory, and God hid Moses in the cleft of the rock and declared his name, Yahweh. That was God's name badge – Yahweh: 'The LORD, the LORD, the compassionate and gracious God, slow to anger, abounding in love and faithfulness, maintaining love to thousands, and forgiving wickedness, rebellion and sin. Yet he does not leave the guilty unpunished.' This is what God had revealed out of his own mouth and Moses says 'Remember these words, remember your own name badge?' Then Moses says in verse 17: 'May the Lord's strength be displayed, just as you have declared.' Literally it says 'May your strength become even greater, magnify and make great your strength, O Lord.'

Moses is saying, 'I understand your anger. But you have an even greater strength because you are Yahweh. You are the God who has the power to forgive and to carry iniquity and to go on being faithful. That's what makes you the God you are. That's your real strength. If you want to be really strong, then carry them and forgive them.'

There is a moment in *Schindler's List* when Schindler speaks to the Nazi who is killing people for sport, and Schindler says 'Yes, that's power, that's strength, but real strength is to show mercy. Real power is when you could kill someone but you choose not to.' It's a very powerful moment that affects the mind of the character for some time. Moses is saying here that God's greatest strength lies not in his power to destroy but his power to forgive.

Israelite families were normally three or four generation families, so if the head of the family falls into idolatry and open sin, then the effect of the sin will affect the whole family within the community in all its three or four generations of living members. But, says God, in Exodus 34:6 and Deuteronomy 7:9–10, what God does in his love is to show love to a *thousand* generations of those who love him. So the ratio of God's forgiving love to his anger is a thousand to one.

These narratives in Numbers show us a characteristic of God that we should not ignore and dare not minimise: his anger against persistent sin and rebellion. It is a terrible reality and these chapters show us this. But the overall story is one of incredible patience and grace. I think it is wrong to simply equate God's love and wrath as equivalent and opposite forces. They are both intrinsic to his divine nature but the Bible repeatedly tells us, in places such as this, that God's love, mercy, kindness and patience outlast his anger. God's reputation and character are the two main points on which Moses appeals to God, but he hints at at least two more that I want to mention briefly. Both of these are more explicit in the Exodus and Deuteronomy versions of the intercessory prayer.

God's promise

In 14:16, he simply mentions the land God promised them on oath. This promise was made to Abraham, and this is clear in Exodus 32 when Moses says to God: 'Turn from your fierce anger; relent and do not bring disaster on your people. Remember your servants Abraham, Isaac and Israel, to whom you swore by your own self' (vs 12-13).

The boldness of Moses astonishes me. It's almost as if Moses is saying 'How can you think such a thing? How can you contemplate destroying all these people? What will that mean for the promise you made to Abraham?' If God can't keep his promise to Abraham, what is the guarantee that he can keep it to Moses? 'How can you expect me to keep on believing you if you abandon one just to make another? Is that the kind of God you are?' Moses is deadly serious with God. Moses goes right to the very character of God; his character, name and very existence.

God's covenant

Verse 19: 'In accordance with your great love, forgive the sin of these people, just as you have pardoned them from the time they left Egypt until now.' Who are these people? 'These are the people that you redeemed, that you brought to yourself, that you bound to yourself at Mount Sinai saying, "They will be my people, I will be their God."' Once again Moses recalls the fact of God's redemption and covenant. In Deuteronomy 9, Moses recalls this in verses 26: 'I prayed to the LORD and said, "O Sovereign LORD, do not destroy your people, your own inheritance that you redeemed by your great power and brought out of Egypt with a mighty hand."'

I'm sure that Moses' response to God saying: 'Look at what your people, whom you brought up out of Egypt, are doing' would be something like, 'Excuse me, God, they're your people and you brought them up out of Egypt.' It's a bold intercession. Moses is asking God to think things through again. He's saying 'Do what you are good at, forgive these people.'

Moses Watch 4: Moses the intercessor

It seems that Moses sets us a wonderful model for the dynamics of intercessory prayer. Moses doesn't try to excuse the people and to call down God's pity. He just goes straight to the things that matter most to God. David tells us in Psalm 138:2 'You have exalted above all things your name and your word.' Moses appeals to the very things that are God's priorities and pleads with God to act to the glory of his name, to act consistently with his own character and in accordance with his promise. This is surely the way we should pray when we pray to God. That is why we say at the end of our prayers, 'For Jesus' sake.'

3. God's punishment and patience (14:20 – 15:2)

God responds to Moses' appeal with a declaration of forgiveness. Verse 20, 'The LORD replied, "I have forgiven them, as you asked."' The intercession has been effective. What does this forgiveness mean? It means that they would not be wiped out instantly. It did not mean that there would be no punishment. God is saying that his plan and purpose would continue through this people; he would not destroy them but he would continue through the next generation. This generation of adults had had their last chance. Their rebellion against God had left God with no alternative but to punish them, and this is what happens.

Punishment

In verses 21-24 we have God's general statement of what is going to happen, and then in verses 26-35 he fills in the specific details. In verses 21-24, God says that

> . . . as surely as the glory of the LORD fills the whole earth, not one of the men who saw my glory and the miraculous signs I performed in Egypt and in the desert but who disobeyed me and tested me ten times–not one of them will ever see the land I promised on oath to their forefathers. No one who has treated me with contempt will ever see it. But because my servant Caleb has a different spirit and follows me wholeheartedly, I will bring him into the land he went to, and his descendants will inherit it.

The contrast in these verses is between what this generation of Israelites had seen and what they would now never see. They had seen all the miracles of God; the Exodus, Sinai, everything that God had done, but they would never see the Promised Land because of their contempt for God and their persistent rebellion. God says this had happened ten times. This could be rhetorical, but actually the Rabbis and Jewish scholars like to look at things like this, and they did in fact come up with ten occasions in Exodus and Numbers which were instances of grumbling, murmuring and rebellion. They pointed to the language of grumbling at the Red Sea (Ex. 14), at Marah (Ex. 15), the Desert of Sinai (three times in Ex. 16), at Rephidim (Ex. 17), at Sinai (Ex. 32), at Taberah (Num. 11:1), at Kibroth (Num. 11:4) and here at Kadesh (Num. 13–14).

This is a tale of constant rejection of God's grace, provision, purposes and love. This is a people who are unrepentantly resistant to God's plan for them. It's no wonder that the apostle Paul uses this story as a dire warning for unbelievers. And he points out that these people had, spiritually speaking, been baptised by Moses: they'd even had an experience of the pre-incarnate Christ in the spiritual rock that followed them and yet, he said, they tested the Lord and were killed. He said that these things happened to them as warnings to us, so that if you think you are standing, you have to be careful that you don't fall.

In verses 26–35 God goes a little further. The point of the contrast here is not just between what the Israelites had *seen* and would never see, but between what the Israelites had *said* and how God takes them at their word. God says in verse 28 'So tell them, "As surely as I live," declares the LORD, "I will do to you the very things I heard you say."' But what had they said?

Earlier in the chapter they'd said, 'We wish we'd died in Egypt or here. We'd rather be dead than go on.' God says, 'Very well, have it your way.' But what they'd also said was that their children would be captured as plunder. That was one of the things that they had said earlier in the chapter. God said, 'No, they won't. They will be shepherded here in the wilderness until all of the parents die off and then they will go in and enjoy the land that you can't have.'

Patience

That moves us from God's punishment to his patience. There is a terrible word that the people respond to, in verse 39, with great mourning and a futile effort at belated obedience. They say 'We'll go up' and they get beaten back, because the Lord isn't with them. It's a terrible word of punishment on the Exodus generation but yet there's still a future for God and God's people. That generation is finished, but God hadn't finished with his plans or the salvation, ultimately, of the world through them. The next 38 years that they were to spend in the wilderness were not to be a stop the clock non-time. Later, when Moses looks back on those years in the wilderness, between this terrible failure and when they reached the brink of crossing into the land, when he is speaking to those who had been children on this day but were now adults, he sees it as a learning experience; an act of parental discipline, when God was trying to teach them something.

In fact, there are two ways we can look at this narrative of Kadesh and the following story of the later generation in the wilderness. We can look at it through the eyes of Psalm 95:10-11 where God says

> 'For forty years I was angry with that generation;
> I said, "They are a people whose hearts go astray,
> and they have not known my ways."
> So I declared on oath in my anger,
> "They shall never enter my rest."'

But look at Moses speaking to the Israelites in Deuteronomy 8:2-3, speaking about the same event. He says

> Remember how the LORD your God led you all the way in the desert these forty years, to humble you and to test you in order to know what was in your heart, whether or not you would keep his commands. He humbled you, causing you to hunger and then feeding you with manna, which neither you nor your fathers had known, to teach you that man does not live on bread alone but on every word that comes from the mouth of the LORD.

God gave them bread to teach them that there were things more important than bread: the word and promise of God. 'Know then in your heart that as a man disciplines his son, so the LORD your God disciplines you' (v5). That's how Moses looks back on it. At one level, it's a huge waste of time, the result of sin and rebellion and yet God turns it into an opportunity for grace and obedience.

It's interesting that in 1 Corinthians 10:11, Paul says that these things were written as a *warning* for us. But in Romans 15:4, Paul says that these things were written for our *learning* 'so that through the endurance and the encouragement of the Scriptures we might have hope.' So where is the encouragement in this passage? It is this: that God turns the wilderness into a time of fresh opportunity to love and trust and obey him. That's what testing means. Even after disobedience God is still there.

Some of us may feel like we are living in a wilderness because of some past act of rebellion or disobedience to God or folly. As a result of that your life feels blighted, and you fall for that nonsense that, if that's the case, you've missed the plan A and you're now in plan B. Don't fall for that. God is patient. You may be in a time of discipline as the Israelites were in the wilderness, but it's not your final destination or where he wants you to stay. There is the place of blessing and the call to renewed blessing and obedience. God can turn the consequences of sin and folly into a response of love and obedience to him, and when we do, God responds with grace and blessing.

Fatal ambition and the judgement of God (4)

Numbers 16

Introduction

There may be times when even the gentlest Christian leader, faced with prolonged hostility and opposition, wishes the earth would open and swallow those who are against him. But in Numbers 16, there is a sustained suspense and terrible final conclusion. This is an awful story and it fills us with horror. It's there as a deadly warning against fatal ambition which can lead to the judgment of God, and yet paradoxically it also points us to the Lord Jesus Christ.

The story interweaves two different rebellions happening at the same time, from different sources and creates a lot of dramatic suspense. It is easy to summarise. There is Korah, who leads a team of Levites in an attack on Moses and Aaron over the issue of priesthood and, at the same time, there is Dathan, Abiram and On, who lead some Reubenites to challenge Moses's authority and to accuse him of domineering over the people. Then God, through Moses, proposes a test in both cases and at the end of the story, the earth opens up and swallows Dathan and Abiram and fire comes out from the tent of the Lord and consumes Korah and his supporters. The whole people complain against God so God strikes them with a plague, which is only finally stopped through the intercession of Moses and the atonement of Aaron. Like the story of the great rebellion, this sticks in the memory of Israel. It's recalled in Psalm 106 and, by Stephen, in Acts 7.

1. Double challenge: motives exposed (16:1-15)

In the first few verses we discover that two groups are involved in this challenge against Moses, although it seems to start out as independent grumbles involving three or four individuals. There is Korah of the Levites and there's Dathan and Abiram of the Reubenites. We know from other descriptions that these two groups lived close to each other in the wilderness. Their tents were together on the south side of the Tabernacle. There are two different complaints but they join forces to make common complaints against the leadership and create serious disaffection at a high level. Verse 2 tells us that this soon involves 250 senior leaders and they were well known. They had been appointed to the council, they had been trusted, and they would certainly have included some of the men who were appointed in Exodus 18. Let's take the two cases separately.

Korah and the Levites: discontent over their status

Korah and the Levites were discontented over their status. (Dathan and Abiram's issue was one of contempt for God's leaders and refusal to accept the leadership that God had appointed.) Verse 3 probably gives us Korah and the Levites' main complaint: 'They came as a group to oppose Moses and Aaron and said to them, "You have gone too far! The whole community is holy, every one of them, and the Lord is with them!"'

They appeal to very plausible scriptural truth, that the whole community of God's people is holy. True. In Exodus 19:6, at Mount Sinai, God had said to the Israelites, 'You will be for me a kingdom of priests and a holy nation.' Israel as a whole was intended to be God's holy people. The narrator intends a flashback to chapter 15:37-41 where God commanded the Israelites to sew tassels onto the hems of their garments so that, even on their clothing, everyone in the community was reminded of their holiness. So, says Korah, 'Why are Aaron and the priests getting a better deal than the rest of us? Why are they being regarded as more holy than anyone else? What's so special about them?' This is jealousy expressing itself as an issue of equality.

The second theological theme that they appeal to is that the Lord is among all the people (v3): 'The Lord is with us.' True. In Exodus 29:45 when Aaron and the Tabernacle had all been consecrated to God, God says 'Then I will dwell among the Israelites and be their God.' The Tabernacle itself was a symbol of the presence of God in the midst of the whole people. Korah says 'God dwells among all of us, so what gives Aaron and the priests special right of access into the presence of God?' Again, it's a demand of equality, based on spiritual truth. But they're ignoring the particular calling and symbolic function that God had laid on Aaron and the priests in the tribe of Levi.

What were they really after? In verses 9-11 Moses, in his response to them, exposes their real motives. Verse 10 contrasts with verse 3

> Isn't it enough for you that the God of Israel has separated you from the rest of the Israelite community and brought you near himself to do the work at the LORD's tabernacle and to stand before the community and minister to them? He has brought you and all your fellow Levites near himself, but now you are trying to get the priesthood too. It is against the LORD that you and all your followers have banded together.

The Levites had a tribal responsibility for the tabernacle, to carry and look after it. They were to serve the people when they came to the Tabernacle and chapter 18 tells us that, in compensation for all this, the Levites got all the tithes from the people. They did not have any inheritance from the land and so they were supported by the gifts of God's people. But within the tribe of Levi, Aaron and his family had a specific priestly responsibility. It was they alone whom God had commissioned to come to the altar to do the manipulation of the blood for the sacrifices: to speak the words of atonement and blessing, to enter once a year into the holy presence of God and many other duties. And the priests had additional duties (Num. 18:8-14).

The Levites (through Korah) were discontented with what God had given them, jealous of what God had given to others (Aaron and sons) and had ambitions for a higher level of authority, and all the perks that went with it. This, said Moses, lay behind all their talk of holiness and the presence of God and everything else. Again, I love Raymond Brown's comment on this: 'They appear to be interested in holiness more as a verbal tag than as a distinctive lifestyle.'[1]

I remember the surprise I had shortly after I was ordained in the Church of England, when someone asked me what were my ambitions and prospects in the ordained ministry. I hadn't even thought about prospects, but he was talking about the career path, the ladder of preferment. I was surprised that people would think of the Christian minister in status terms. Those who travel the world see that this afflicts the church wherever we go. Even where we rejoice at the phenomenal growth of the church, we find exactly this same problem – people wanting status and prestige in Christian ministry.

Dathan and Abiram: contempt for God's leaders

It's probable that the second half of verse 3 is Dathan and Abiram's complaint, where it says 'Why then do you set yourselves above the LORD's assembly?' In other words, 'Who gave you the right to be in charge?' There is a tension between the equality of all God's people and the God-appointed role and necessity that there should be leaders. It's a tension that God's people have never seemed to get quite right. But there's much more than a theological conflict. Moses summons these people in verse 12 and says 'Let's sort this out' but they wouldn't. Then in verses 13-14 you get the perverse and defiant accusations against Moses: 'Isn't it enough that you have brought us up out of a land filled with milk and honey to kill us in the desert? And now you also want to lord it over us?' They attribute to Moses the same evil intention that they had attributed to God: 'You brought us up to kill us in the desert. That's what you want, isn't it, Moses? You want us all dead. You want to lord it over us.'

Why were these people not going into a land of milk and honey? It wasn't because Moses didn't lead them there; it was the people who refused. Here you have this perversity of the people who attribute their own failure to the leadership of the people.

Moses Watch 5: human anger (v15)

I sometimes used to compare being a leader among God's people to being blotting paper. Blotting paper mops up spilt ink. Sometimes that's what leaders have to do. But this makes Moses very angry. We're told in 12:3 that Moses was a very humble man. So what was it that sparked this reaction?

I think that it was the last phrase of verse 13 where they accuse him of 'wanting to lord it over us.' The first time Moses had heard these words was forty years ago in Egypt, when he had tried to help his own people by killing an Egyptian (Ex. 2:14). That had led to forty years in the wilderness for Moses. Now these people had been so rebellious that Moses is going to have to spend another forty years in the wilderness with them. And the tune still hasn't changed. They still accuse him of wanting to 'lord it over them.' Moses knew deep in his heart that he would rather be anywhere else except in this position of leadership. This was an unjust accusation against him. And he becomes very angry, and protests to God against this accusation, which he feels is so unforgivably unfair. He says 'I haven't even stolen a donkey from them' – a typical Jewish way of declaring your own innocence. He's saying 'Lord, I've done nothing to deserve this kind of accusation.' And he says 'Don't forgive them, don't accept their offering.'

This is the same man who, in Exodus 32:32, asked God to block his name out of the Book of Life rather than destroy anyone, who had pleaded with God to forgive the people for the rebellion (Num. 14). But Moses is a man of flesh and blood and he explodes with anger.

2. Double test: verdict delivered

The narrator goes on to interweave what happens to Korah and the Levite supporters with what happens with Dathan, Abiram and his Reubenite supporters. The story gets confusing at times but the main events are clear.

Korah and the Levites: whom does God accept? (vs 5-7, 16-19, 35-40)

Korah and the Levites said that they were as holy as the priests. Moses jumps to the defence of Aaron, his brother who had been in opposition to him earlier. He proposes a test (vs 16-19). He says 'Bring your censers. Light your fires, burn the incense and let's see if God accepts you.' What happens? Verse 35: 'fire came out from the LORD and consumed the 250 men who were offering the incense.' The verdict is then made plain (v40): 'This was to remind the Israelites that no one except a descendant of Aaron should come to burn incense before the LORD, or he would become like Korah and his followers.'

Dathan and Abiram: whom has God appointed? (vs 25-34)

The second verdict is delivered on Dathan and Abiram right in the middle of the story of Korah, to build up the suspense. First of all, God tells Moses to warn the Israelites to separate themselves from these defiant rebels. Notice how they persisted in their defiance. Verse 27: 'So they [the people] moved away from the tents of Korah, Dathan and Abiram. Dathan and Abiram had come out and were standing with their wives, children and little ones at the entrance to the tents.'

Verses 28-30 are important to the way in which Moses describes the actual conflict: 'This is how you will know that the LORD has sent me to do all these things and that it was not my idea.' Moses passes the decision on to God. Moses says let God show the truth. The truth is two-fold: positively that 'God sent me' and negatively, 'This is not my idea. This has all come from the will, purpose and plan of God.' Moses' authority and plan of action have all come from the work of God, and Moses says 'You need to know who it is that you are really opposing. You are showing contempt for God, not just for me.'

The act of judgment was immediate and extraordinary (vs 31-34): 'the ground under them split apart and the earth opened its mouth and swallowed them.' The whole household of these men went alive into the grave. Part of the horror of the story is that the God who created the earth for our blessing and enjoyment uses it as the ground for his awesome judgement. In both cases, God acted to defend what he had established; Aaron's unique priesthood and Moses' unique authority. Neither of them vindicated themselves: God made his verdict unmistakable.

It is possible for a story like this to be abused by unscrupulous leaders of God's people who are guilty of the kind of tyrannical monopolising of power and status that Moses was *not* guilty of. I hesitate to apply this story because I know it can be abused by self-appointed leaders. They say, 'Don't oppose me or God will destroy you!' It becomes an oppressive form of manipulation and subjecting others to one's own claimed authority. When you think about it, the Bible shows us that leaders can be far more of a problem to God's people than a help. A lot of the leaders in the Old and New Testament end by showing us just how weak, sinful and sometimes stupid they can be.

The American branch of Langham Partnership, the John Stott Ministries, has as its strap line 'Developing strategic Christian leaders worldwide.' I remember sitting at dinner once with John Goldingay. He said 'I have problems with that line. Don't you think that in the Bible leaders are the problem, not the solution? Isn't it often the leaders who are the great dividers of God's people, who lead God's people astray? Shouldn't we be developing strategic *servants* among God's people?' I had to agree with him.

We need to see the unique role of Moses and Aaron within the Bible history of salvation. These are unique men and in different ways stand as a type of the Lord Jesus Christ. Certainly we need to be careful about putting ourselves in opposition against those who are in leadership over God's people. We are to challenge those leaders who go astray, that's what the prophets were sent for, but Paul tells is that we should do that with gentleness and respect, speaking the truth in love.

3. Double intercession: atonement provided

Moses prays like Abraham (v22)

There is one more feature of this narrative that needs mentioning. Three times in this one chapter Moses falls on his face (vs 4, 22, 45). Twice in this chapter Moses specifically intercedes with God, pleading for mercy and seeking to provide atonement. On both occasions in verses 21 and 45, God speaks identical words: 'Get away from these people and I will destroy them utterly.' In verse 22, Moses acts in response to that when he prays like Abraham: 'O God, God of the Spirit of all mankind, will you be angry with the entire assembly when only one man sins?' He appeals to the justice of God, just as Abraham did when he interceded for Sodom and Gomorrah (in Gen. 18), that God should act appropriately and not punish the whole of God's people for the offence of a few.

Moses intercedes with God on the basis of his known character. He's the God of all people, the God of justice and so Moses says 'You must judge, but let your judgement be discriminating on those who are truly the offenders.' Verse 41, 'The next day the whole Israelite community grumbled against Moses and Aaron. "You have killed the LORD's people," they said.' Both aspects of the accusations were not true. It wasn't Moses or Aaron who had killed anyone; it was God who had acted without human agency. And Korah, Dathan and Abiram, by their actions, had ceased to be part of the Lord's people – they had set themselves up as enemies of God. The tragedy in the Old Testament is that the whole people of Israel would discover what it would mean to have God as their enemy and to be treated no longer as his people.

Notice there is an awesome and fearless escalation of sin. This started with Korah, then it becomes a gang of four (with Dathan, Abiram and On) and then all 250 of the leaders. A day later it had become the whole of Israel. There is something frightfully infectious about sin.

Moses acts through Aaron (vs 41-50)

In verse 45 God threatens total destruction and in verse 46 Moses acts, no longer only in prayer. Moses sent Aaron, Israel's great High Priest, the one whom God himself had appointed to stand in the gap and to atone for his people, and Aaron physically puts himself between the people of God and the wrath of God. The language of atonement is spoken of twice (vs 46,47). It's the same word that is used in the context of the sacrifices mentioned in Leviticus, when it speaks of both the cleansing away of sin and the averting of the wrath of God from the sinner. Aaron, here as elsewhere, is a symbolic portrait of the work of the Lord Jesus Christ.

What do we learn from a story like this? We learn the severity of God's judgment on unrepentant, defiant, persistent rebellion against him. There is something exemplary about this which give us a picture of the seriousness of sin and points to the final judgment of God – as do the flood, the story of Sodom and Gomorrah, the destruction of the wicked Canaanites and the New Testament story of Ananias and Sapphira; stories which are intentionally symbolic.

Don't continue this false dichotomy that says the Old Testament God is the God of wrath and the God of the New Testament is a God of mercy. The wrath and mercy of God are in both Testaments. Therefore what we see finally is the uniqueness of God's atonement. The emphasis in the concluding verse is that only Aaron can function as the High Priest, and that's confirmed in chapter 17 through the budding of Aaron's staff, proving that this is the one whom God has chosen to stand as his atoning agent. Moses prefigures the Lord Jesus in intercession and Aaron prefigures him in atonement. At this point in their history, Aaron was the only one who could make atonement for all Israel, and we know from the Scriptures that Jesus is the only one appointed by God who can make atonement for all the world and all humanity. The Lamb of God who takes away the sin of the world. Let's give thanks then to God for his grace.

Endnotes

[1] Raymond Brown, *The Message of Numbers* (IVP: BST series, Nottingham, 2002)

Curses, blessings and the protection of God (5)
Numbers 22-25

Introduction

This chapter is filled with surprise, irony, humour, and contrasts, and is extremely well told. The background is that the two kings of the Amorites, Sihon and Og, have been defeated. The Israelites had asked to go through their countries but the kings had come out and attacked the Israelites and were defeated. So Moab, the kingdom where the Israelites were camping at that point, was scared, and Balak, the king of Moab, feels that his country is going to be devastated by this moving horde of Israelites that have come out of the wilderness, though in fact God had told them not to attack Moab or take any of their land (Deut. 2:9).

Balak knows that he can't defeat them in battle so he decides to turn to sorcery and sends for the best magician around, Balaam, the son of Beor. It takes about three weeks to get there and three weeks to get back and they had to do the journey twice, so it took Balak more than three months to get this speaker. Balaam is a historical character. Texts found on the walls of an ancient sanctuary in northern Jordan in 1967 refer to Balaam son of Beor, a seer of the gods. He was a soothsayer and would do a good line in whatever you wanted to pay him for.

1. Balak and his bright idea (22:1-6)

In verse 6, we get the first hint of irony. Balak says 'I know that those you bless are blessed, and those you curse are cursed.' But the only one who has the authority to say that is the God of Abraham; Balaam is a pagan seer. That doesn't stop God intervening in his life and using him.

Balaam and this puzzling God (22:7-20)

We know this God as Yahweh but Balaam saw him as another god that he was going to have to manipulate in some way. In verses 7-20, Balak's messengers arrive and bring their fee. It's late, so they stay the night. Then the first touch of humour (v9). God says, 'Who's this that's come into your house?' Balaam tells him: 'I've heard from someone called Balak, king of Moab, that this people have come out of Egypt and landed in his back yard.' You can imagine God saying 'Tell me about it. I didn't know about this!'

The humour here is like on the road to Emmaus where Jesus asks the two men what's been happening in Jerusalem and they say 'Are you the only person who doesn't know what's been happening?' Jesus, who has been crucified and raised from the dead – the one who was the whole focus of attention in Jerusalem that weekend – says, 'What's been going on?'

God gives to Balaam two clear instructions (v12): 'You must not go . . .' and 'You must not put a curse on those people, because they are blessed.' The next morning Balaam gives an answer to the embassy from Moab, but he only gives half of God's answer. He says 'God has told me not to come.' He doesn't tell them that God has told him not to curse.

So the men go back to Balak and report the answer (v14). Balak doesn't know Balaam has been told not to curse, so thinks it's just a question of a higher fee. So he sends a higher offer. Balaam gives a remarkable reply (v18). He says that 'Even if Balak gives me his palace filled with silver and gold, I could not do anything great or small to go beyond the command of the LORD my God.' Is this pagan seer genuinely talking like this? Or is this a safety clause in the contract that he hopes he can waive later on? God says (v20) 'Go, but make sure you only do what I tell you.'

The angel and the two stubborn asses (22:21-35)

Verse 22 is puzzling. Balaam saddles his donkey and sets off but God is very angry. Why? God told him to go. The only explanation is that God perceived that Balaam's intention in going was wrong. He might have been thinking 'I've been told by God not to curse, but let's see what happens.' Balaam makes his living by manipulating gods and spirits to do whatever purpose he gets paid for, and so he's probably expecting that, when the time comes, he'll be able to do the same thing this time, and to collect the biggest fee from the richest customer he has ever had, the king of Moab.

This is what I deduce from the combination of verses 20 and 35. Notice after the incident with the angel and the donkey (v35), God says again what he'd said before, 'Go with the men, but speak only what I tell you,' as if to say that when Balaam set off for the first time, he'd not mentally agreed to that. There was some get-out clause in his mind.

God sends his angel to oppose Balaam, and the comedy with the donkey begins. Three times in the story the angel of God, with a drawn sword, stands in front of Balaam and the donkey. Balaam doesn't see the angel but the donkey does, and three times the donkey tries to avoid taking action. First time he can actually get off the road and runs away. Second time he's between two walls of a vineyard and he moves aside and crushes Balaam's foot against the wall. Third time he can't go forward or back and so squats down and won't move on until Balaam beats him three times and makes him move on.

In verses 28-30, we have God opening the mouth of the donkey. The donkey protests: 'What have I done to you to make you beat me these three times?' Balaam says, 'You've made a fool of me and I'd kill you now if I could.' As Peter Lewis puts it 'the narrator inserts mockery into history through the mouth of this donkey.'

The narrator piles irony upon irony in this part of the story. Think of the number of contrasts happening here. The man on the donkey is called a seer, but he can't see what's in front of his eyes; the donkey sees what the seer can't. Balaam gets paid to be eloquent: this dumb animal gets beaten until he's the one who talks first. The donkey turns aside from the way his master wants him to go, as Balaam is intent on doing. Balaam gets angry with the donkey: God is angry with Balaam. Balaam says he would kill the donkey if only he had a sword in his hand instead of a stick: the angel, who does have a sword in his hand, says that it is only the donkey that saves Balaam's life. Balaam is trying to get the donkey to do what Balak is trying to get Balaam to do – what he wants. Balaam tries beating, Balak tries bribing. The results are equally ineffective.

Balak, the king of Moab, is blind to the reality of the God that he's dealing with: so is Balaam until God opens his eyes. The donkey sees the angel of God and then God opens its mouth. Eventually Balaam, God's other ass in the story, is led to see the revelation of God and compelled to speak God's words. By the end of this section in verse 35, Balaam is being reminded of what the angel first said to him, which is, 'Go with these men, but speak only what I tell you.' Balaam has been frightened and mocked into obedience. The story is set on course for a clash of intentions and perspectives. Balaam can do nothing but what God tells him to do, and Balak cannot get Balaam to do anything that he wants him to do.

Balak and his cash for curses (22:36 – 23:6)

In verses 22:36-23:6 Balaam arrives. Balak gets angry: 'Didn't I send for you? Why didn't you come? Am I not able to reward you?' In verse 38, Balaam says 'I am here now, look at my injured foot. But I can only speak what God puts in my mouth.' Then they go to the high places, offer the right sacrifices, get a good view, make sure that everything is in order, and then the message begins to come (Num. 23:5).

2. Blessings for main course (23 – 24:19)

If you hire some famous provider, you expect to get what you pay for. If you go to an expensive restaurant, you expect to choose what you pay for. Balak chooses curses for his main course, but it's as if Balaam says 'Sorry, curses are off today. I can do you blessings or blessings. You can have them boiled, fried, however you want them, but it has to be blessings.'

What's the point of this story? Unknown to them as yet, the people of God are under attack from external enemies, those they didn't know. Equally unknown to them, God is protecting them, and turning every effort to curse them into blessing. Isn't this remarkable when you think of the stories we've been thinking of? Here are people who still live under the overarching protection of God, under his promise and blessing. This does not mean they will never sin or be attacked again. The rest of the history of the Old Testament and indeed the church is of attacks on God's people, of persecution, violence, suffering and everything else. But what the oracles of Balaam declare is the ultimate security and blessing of God's people. These oracles have the same purpose as those in Ezekiel against Gog and Magog (Ezek. 38-39) which also speaks about how God will ultimately protect his people from their enemies, whoever they may be. And Revelation speaks of the protective presence and ministry of God, with his suffering people.

What we have in this chapter are four main oracles, interspersed by desperate attempts by Balak to get Balaam to find a curse or two. It's poetic. The blessings and the oracles are very symbolic. They're figurative and futuristic in some sense, so need very careful interpretation. I want to point out a key point in each oracle and to observe the overall message that God's people will remain secure because of four distinct truths of what God promises them.

Oracle 1 – God's Abrahamic protection (23:7-11)

Balaam says 'How can I curse those whom God has not cursed? How can I denounce those whom God has not denounced?' Why can he not? Because these are the people whom God had promised in his blessing with Abraham (Gen. 12:3): 'I will bless those who bless you, and whoever curses you I will curse.' Old Testament Israel was protected by this promise.

There is a further hint at this in verse 10 as Balaam says 'Who can count the dust of Jacob or number the fourth part of Israel?' This reference to the dust of the people is clearly an echo of 13:16. God promised Abraham that his descendants would be as numerous as the sand on the shore, the dust on the earth and the stars in the sky. Here are a people who stand under the protection of God because of what God has promised to Abraham. Israel in the Old Testament is unique: in another word from Balaam (v9): 'From the rocky peaks I see them, from the heights I view them. I see a people who live apart and do not consider themselves one of the nations.' This doesn't mean that the Israelites are hermits or that there's exclusiveness here. God is saying that he has done things to and for Israel that he has done for no other nation. This is affirmed in Deuteronomy and elsewhere.

Why are these people unique? Why is God doing this? Back to Abraham again; it is for the sake of the nations, and ultimately for the blessings of the nations. This is God's mission, which is why he makes these promises and provides this protection. Balaam is so impressed with this first oracle that he wishes he could share it. 'Let me die the death of the righteous, and may my end be like theirs!' Tragically, he did not (Num. 31:8).

Oracle 2 – God's redeeming presence (23:13-26)

Just before the second oracle, Balak tries again to get things properly arranged. Maybe this time he will be able to manipulate this God, whoever he is, into a change of mind. But God says that this is not possible (v19). In verses 18-20 Balaam utters his oracle, 'Arise, Balak, and listen; hear me, son of Zippor. God is not a man, that he should lie, nor a son of man, that he should change his mind. Does he speak and then not act? Does he promise and not fulfil? I have received a command to bless; he has blessed, and I cannot change it.'

Verse 21 is a little puzzling in its first half, but is made a little clearer in the second half. 'No misfortune is seen in Jacob, no misery observed in Israel.' That's surprising. Perhaps it means that in spite of all the problems, Israel will survive. Or perhaps the NIV is right in the footnote translation that says 'God has not looked on Jacob's offences or the wrongs that are found in Israel.' They are there but God will ultimately cleanse and forgive them.

The real point of this second oracle comes in the second half of verse 21 and verse 22. 'The LORD their God is with them; the shout of the king is among them. God brought them up out of Egypt; they have the strength of a wild ox.' God has brought these people up out of Egypt and now he's among them as the victorious king. Balaam says (v23), 'There is no sorcery against Jacob, no divination against Israel. It will now be said of Jacob and of Israel, "See what God has done!"' The salvation and the redemption and all that God has done for these people is God's work, and Balaam says 'I can't stand against them, it's the work of God.' God's people are secure: God is their King (v21), their Redeemer (v22) and their Protector (v23).

Oracle 3 – God's abundant provision (23:27 – 24:14)

This time Balaam doesn't even bother with divination and sorcery. He begins to realise what he's up against. Chapter 24 begins, 'Now when Balaam saw that it pleased the LORD to bless Israel, he did not resort to sorcery as at other times, but turned his face toward the desert. When Balaam looked out and saw Israel encamped tribe by tribe, the Spirit of God came upon him and he uttered his oracle' (vs 1-3). God has been speaking through Balaam up to this point, but what the narrator makes very clear here is that he is speaking by the Spirit of the living God.

The last time we saw the Spirit of God was in chapter 11 when we heard that the Spirit was on Moses, then God had taken that Spirit and put it on the seventy elders to prophesy. Here the Spirit comes on a pagan seer. God is not limited in those he can speak through. And this third oracle is the speech of God directly from the Spirit.

The first oracle was about the past, the promise of God to Abraham. The second oracle was closer to the present because it refers to the Exodus and the Sinai experience, and how God is in the midst of these people. This third oracle (and the fourth) look much more into the future, and the blessing and the peace that is going to come to this people. God's people will be secure because of God's abundant provision for them. Look at 24:5-7: 'How beautiful are your tents, O Jacob, your dwelling-places, O Israel! Like valleys they spread out, like gardens beside a river, like aloes planted by the LORD, like cedars beside the waters. Water will flow from their buckets; their seed will have abundant water.'

It's a beautiful picture. The word for 'beautiful' is translated by the NIV as 'good'; it's the word that we heard in chapter 10 when Moses had said to Hobab 'God has promised good things to Israel.' We return to the good that even Balaam can see as he looks to the people. This is a picture of peace, prosperity and abundance, and at one level it's poetic: it points towards an ideal picture of Canaan to which Israel went and centuries later was going to lose because of their sin.

We also need to recognise that the picture of the land points forward into other directions as well. In the New Testament, the land points forward to the Lord Jesus Christ, as does everything. In the New Testament, we discover that the land of Israel is no longer significant as territory but rather it is taken up into what we now have in Christ. The one thing that we do not have, says the writer to the Hebrews, 'is an earthly city.' We become citizen of God's country, have a place in God's own family, a place of God's own dwelling in the temple of God, using all the imagery of land and house and temple and uniting Gentiles and Jews together in Christ.

But also the Old Testament teaching on the land points beyond that to a new creation. Many pictures in the prophets speak even more eloquently than Balaam does here of the new heaven and the new earth and of God dwelling with his people in that new creation. This third oracle points to the land that Israel would go to, the abundant provision that God would make for his people.

Oracle 4 – God's Messianic promise (24:15-25)

This comes after some frustrated anger from Balak (24:10-11): 'He struck his hands together and said to him, "I summoned you to curse my enemies, but you have blessed them these three times. [Just as Balaam had beaten his donkey three times.] Now leave at once and go home! I said I would reward you handsomely, but the LORD has kept you from being rewarded."' Balaam says 'I'm sorry, I told you that. I said that I wasn't going to be able to bring anything but blessings, and now I'm going to warn you about what you and the Moabites can expect in the future.' This fourth oracle runs from verses 15-25 and it's God's messianic promise. The key verse is verse 17. Balaam says 'I see him, but not now; I behold him, but not near. A star will come out of Jacob; a sceptre will rise out of Israel. He will crush the foreheads of Moab.'

In Old Testament history, there is no doubt that as these oracles of Balaam were recorded and eventually passed on, this would have been seen as referring to King David, who did subdue Moab and the other kingdoms. A sceptre, a king, arose in Israel who did exactly what Balaam had said. But as we look at this verse and the great sweep of biblical history, it also points forward to David's greater Son, the one who came as the Messiah King, to Jesus who brought with him the reign of God, not just over Israel but ultimately over all the nations of the world.

These four oracles have taken us from the distant past to the distant future, from Abraham to the Messiah. In this inspired poetry of a soothsayer, God, through his Spirit, spreads before us his whole counsel. What we have here is God's promise to Abraham and his blessing on Israel for the sake of the whole world.

Secondly, Balaam has spoken about God's redemption of his people, the Exodus which prefigures the cross, as the New Testament teaches us. Having redeemed his people, God remains present among them. Thirdly, he's spoken about God's provision for his people, both in this world and the world to come. Fourthly, he has mentioned God's messianic reign, the one who would come in the form of David but ultimately in the servant messianic kingship of Christ. What a declaration of the ultimate security of God's people!

3. Tragedy for afters (Num. 25)

But what temptation and idolatry followed afterwards! That's the horror of the story.

God was able to protect Israel from the cursing of their external enemies, but he couldn't deflect them from the lust that was in their own hearts. And Balaam had a part in this. We're not told this in this story, it's almost as if the narrator doesn't want to put that in here, but we do know from Numbers 31:15-16 that the women of Moab were following Balaam's advice and they were the means of turning the Israelites away from the Lord.

Conclusion

The overall lesson is one of blessing, protection and security for the people of God.

Now, you may have noticed that throughout I have used the expression 'Old Testament Israel' quite frequently, referring to the fact that the people that Balaam was speaking about were the people of God in the Old Testament, people who had been called into existence, saved from slavery, privileged with the knowledge of God, entrusted with God's covenant and law and promises, called the household of God, the family of God and the people of God in the Old Testament.

But the Old Testament itself repeatedly foretells and the New Testament teaches clearly and explicitly that *in Christ* the Israel of God is redefined and extended to include no longer an ethnic or territorial state or city – ancient or modern, but the multi-national family of God, believing Jews and Gentiles, drawn from every language, people and tribe. These prophecies of Balaam, along with all the other prophecies and promises of the Old Testament, are part of those promises of God that are the 'Yes and Amen of God.' So it is biblically and theologically right to see the promises of these chapters as intended for God's people down through history – including ourselves as the people of God in Christ.

There is not a suggestion in the rest of Numbers that the sin of the people in chapter 25 somehow cancels out all the chapters of great blessing and promise in chapters 23 and 24. The people of God, the church in the power of the Spirit, remains a community of failed sinners. But this is still the community of God's people who trust in God's protection, vision and promise.

Our hearts have been torn this week by the suffering in Lebanon and Israel, and we've been praying for God to protect his ancient people, the Arab and Jewish people. I also know that there are many here who are serving God in cross-cultural mission in the tough places in the world. Many are fearful for the church in the countries where you live, where the Christians are young in faith, vulnerable and few. I want to encourage you that God's words of promise and protection are also given for those people. This doesn't mean that we never suffer persecution or death or danger, but it does mean that the Lord knows those who are his, and he will protect them for eternity.

> For I am convinced that neither death nor life, neither angels nor demons, neither the present nor the future, nor any powers, neither height nor depth, nor anything else in all creation, will be able to separate us from the love of God that is in Christ Jesus our Lord (Rom. 8:38-39).

The words of Paul lead us in no doubt whatsoever. We have a sure foundation for our faith and hope and future.

The Lecture

Week 3: The place of Apologetics in a post-modern culture

by Amy Orr-Ewing

Amy Orr-Ewing

Amy Orr-Ewing is Training Director of the Zacharias Trust. She gained a first class degree in Theology at Christ Church, Oxford, before receiving a Masters degree in Theology at King's College, London. As well as overseeing the Trust's apologetics training programme, Amy is invited to speak at many universities, churches and conferences. She has co-authored (with her husband) and contributed to several books and her book, *Why trust the Bible?* was shortlisted for the 2006 Christian Book Awards. Amy has travelled widely, including visits to Afghanistan, China and South Africa. She is married to Frog (Francis) who is a vicar in the Church of England, and they live in London with their twin boys.

The place of Apologetics in a post-modern culture

What do you think when you hear the words 'a post-modern culture'? It's difficult to define but at a very basic level, post-modernism is simply the worldview which has replaced the worldview of modernism. The modern world had a belief in human progress, science and absolute truths that were discoverable and able to be communicated. That modern world has begun to be displaced by what is known as post-modernism. Post-modernism isn't something tangible: it's more a response and reaction to what has gone before.

The best word to sum up post-modernism is disillusionment: a disillusionment with the ideals of the modern world, of human progress, of the idea or ideal of absolute truth, and alongside this disillusionment a questioning and cynicism about truth and reality.

This is the context we live in: a sense that there aren't answers to the difficult questions we face: that truth is a relative thing. David Bowie was interviewed in the *Sunday Times* magazine and he said these words, which sum up the post-modern world: 'John Lennon, Pete Townsend and I all had this same thing of rather cobbling together one's own belief system – in my case, one that changes all the time as I need to change it. Because I cannot really come to grips with absolutism. I'm fascinated by characters like Thomas More. I think it's because it is so alien to how I seem to cope with life. I can't understand how people can be like that. They are exotic creatures to me.

How do they get to that place where they know with absolute certainty what's true?'[1]

This is the post-modern culture and context in which we are teaching Christ crucified. We are preaching to a culture that is only certain of one thing: that you can't be certain about anything. We are preaching to a world that is struggling to hear the message of the gospel, and this is where apologetics comes in.

How should we share the gospel?

I Peter 3:15: 'But in your hearts set apart Christ as Lord. Always be prepared to give an answer to everyone who asks you to give the reason for the hope that you have. But do this with gentleness and respect, keeping a clear conscience, so that those who speak maliciously against your good behaviour in Christ may be ashamed of their slander.'

It's here in the Greek that we hear the word *apologia*, from which we get the word 'apologetics.' Often people think that my job is to apologise to people. In verse 15, the word is translated as 'answer', and this is the word that the Bible translators have given. *Apologia* means a reasoned defence, a legal defence used in the Greek law courts, or simply an answer. So what is Peter telling us as the church?

It's for everyone

Peter is speaking to the saints and the whole church that have been scattered through persecution. He's not writing to a group of especially intellectual people, he's speaking to all of us.

Holiness

The context of this demand is one of holiness. Peter has been talking about how to live out your life amidst persecution: 'Always be prepared to give an answer when people ask you.' The assumption is that we are living qualitatively different lives from those around us; demonstrating the reality of Christ in the way we live so that our lives will cause people to ask questions.

Get fit

We see the word *gymnasia* here, from which we get 'gymnastics,' physical activity. Peter is saying 'Get fit, get ready, so that when your life calls forth questions, you will find yourself able to give an answer.'

Nine months ago I gave birth to two boys and they weighed quite a lot. At the end of my pregnancy my tummy was huge. Having given birth, it was very hard to embrace getting fit again. It doesn't just happen, it takes work. Peter is saying we need to be prepared, and to get fit is going to take work.

Use reason

Peter uses the word *logion* – reason. This is the word from which we get the word logic. He is saying that when your life calls forth questions from other people, you're to give an answer and to use reason and logic in that answer. There is to be a content to the gospel that you are proclaiming. The gospel is bigger than your personal experience, and the gospel is capable of being explained to people, so that people can listen to your explanation and it will make sense. Peter is saying that you need to explain Christ and his cross in a way that connects with people.

The Zacharias Trust, the organisation I work for, was founded by an Indian man called Ravi Zacharias. One of our colleagues in India is L. T. Jeyachandran, and he is a wonderful Christian man. He used to be a high ranking government official before he came to work for our ministry. In India that meant that he had a driver who drove him to his appointments. He said that the appearance of black cats (which mean bad luck) would throw his drivers into difficulties. One would wind down his window and spit out on the road, somehow undoing the curse of the cat by spitting. Another would see the cat crossing, drive over where it had been, put the car in reverse and drive over it again, somehow undoing the curse. The third driver saw the cat coming and would slow down in anticipation of the cat and let another car overtake, thereby getting the curse on his behalf.

We call these beliefs superstitions: there is no reason to believe that a black cat will bring you bad luck. Peter is saying that the gospel is not a superstition: it has a logic, a reason, and the reason is Christ's cross. The cross is capable of being explained, in the most simple way. In fact Jesus said 'You must become a child to enter into the kingdom of heaven.'

My god-daughter (who's about five years old) and I went off for a walk. She took me into a chapel where there was an iron cross. She said to me 'Look at that cross. Jesus died for our sins on that cross.' Even as a five year old, she has understood something of the cross. It was capable of being explained. Yet the cross is so profound and incredible that the greatest minds that ever lived cannot plumb the depths of what took place. It is so profound that the problems of suffering and evil find their resolution on the cross. The *logion* for what we believe is the cross of Christ.

Be gentle

Finally, we are to engage in apologetics in a particular manner. Peter says we must do it 'with gentleness and respect, keeping a clear conscience.' He's saying that when people ask you, the manner in which you speak is very important. Your gentleness and respect for that person, your attitude is an integral part of your apologetic, and your life is an integral part.

People often say that Christians are hypocrites. Why do you think that Peter says 'keep a clear conscience'? He's not saying that you have to live a perfect life in order to engage in evangelism, he's saying 'Have a short account with God, make sure that you bring your life under the gaze of Jesus and that you confess your sins regularly.'

My husband's family live in South Africa, and many of them are not Christians. One of the churches that invited us to speak had a very sad occurrence whereby the pastor ended up having an affair with a lady in the church. He was kicked out of the ministry and it made front page news. One of my husband's uncles immediately rang us up and said 'See, Christians are hypocrites!' Peter says here, 'Christians, bring your life under the gaze of Jesus, be involved in evangelism but make sure that your life has been brought under Jesus' gaze.'

Apologetics is about giving answers to people's questions, responding to the questions that our postmodern world is raising. Jesus spent a huge amount of time in conversation with individuals. In John's gospel there is a whole series of conversations. John 1 is all about Jesus' conversation with his first disciples, John 2 is the turning of the water into wine and Jesus' conversation with Mary, John 3 is Jesus talking to Nicodemus, John 4 is a conversation between Jesus and the woman at the well. John 6 is a series of conversations between Jesus and his disciples, John 9 is conversations between Jesus and the man born blind. He spent time talking to individuals, and this task of evangelism and apologetics is as simple as that. It's following Christ and spending time in conversations with individuals.

Throughout these conversations, Jesus does one thing time and time again. He asks people questions. Michael Ramsden has counted that Jesus asks 157 questions. He spends time talking with individuals and asks them questions. How do you feel about doing that? Apologetics for us, in a postmodern culture, specifically involves talking to people who aren't Christians. I want to give you three examples of conversations that have come up again and again, to help you in your conversation with friends and neighbours.

Outright aggression

A few years ago I was involved in a mission at Cambridge University, based at one of the colleges. What sometimes happens at these mission events is that the CU get excited beforehand about doing evangelism and then, when the week comes, all the Christians disappear! The CU in the college was only about five people and four of them disappeared. The one who didn't disappear lived quite a compromised life, but she at least had some non-Christian friends, and so on the first night she took me into the college bar. We were at the bar ordering when someone walked up to us. She introduced me to him: 'This is Amy and she's come to stay in the college this week as part of the Christian mission.'

He turned white with rage, and he laid into me: 'How dare you be here. You are a ****! I believe that Christianity is a load of *****! It is outrageous that you enforce your opinions on us!' Other people were stunned by the reaction and all eyes were on us. I remembered that Jesus had conversations with people and asked questions. I said 'Why do you feel so strongly about it?' He said 'Christianity is a load of rubbish. I'm in the choir and have been to church every day of my life. I know that it's there's nothing in it.'

I thought 'I'm a vicar's daughter and a vicar's wife and he's been to church more than me. This is worrying!' There was a silence as I thought what to say, and he said 'Why are you here anyway?' I said, 'I'm here because I believe that it's true and I want you to have an opportunity to respond. There are lots of reasons for why I'm a Christian but I want to give you just two. I believe that Christianity has the answers of the human heart and that it is intellectually verifiable. It not only makes sense, it is real.' He said, 'What do you mean, it is intellectually verifiable?' We went on to talk about history and the gospel and the resurrection for about four hours. At the end of that conversation, he said 'Why has no one ever told me this before? I've never had a conversation with a Christian.' Try asking questions like Jesus did; try getting to the heart and root of why that person is so angry and aggressive.

It's all a matter of interpretation

'How can you say that you have the truth if you Christians all disagree about things?' Interestingly, we're beginning to hear this in the church too. This idea comes from post-modernism, and one of the big philosophical ideas about post-modernism is that it's all a matter of interpretation. People like Derrida and Foucault have written philosophical books, and have said that there is no God; therefore there is no fixed meaning for language.

My husband Frog is a clergyman and has a lot of school friends who are not Christians. Because he is the only vicar they know, he gets invited to do a lot of weddings. About three years ago he was invited to do a smart wedding and decided to preach a real hell-fire gospel message. After this, we were both at the reception talking to a couple there. Around three minutes into the conversation, the husband said to me: 'I can't lie to you. Before we came, my girlfriend and I decided to swap lives. Since I'm a management consultant and my girlfriend works in the arts, we thought we would swap and see if people would react differently to us when we told them what we did. But I can't lie to you; why do you think that is?'

We had a wonderful conversation about the reason for the hope within. Halfway through, he said 'I wonder whether my girlfriend has managed to deceive your husband, the vicar.' It turned out that the girlfriend had said exactly the same thing to Frog and they'd fallen into conversation about Jesus. Her big question was one of interpretation. 'At university I have learnt from all the post-modern writers that since there is no God who is outside reality, language has no reference point outside the words, therefore they only have the meaning that the reader or the listener gives them. When I pick up a book, I look at the words on the page. They don't speak to me; they only have the meaning that is already inside my head. It's just my interpretation. I make the meaning when people speak to me because I'm the listener.' This is a key classic plank of post-modern thought. Words have no reference point outside reality so they can have no intrinsic meaning.

She said 'I went along to a *Christianity Explored* meeting and I was intrigued about Jesus, but I realised that I was putting my meaning on the text. It's a matter of interpretation.' Friedrich Nietzsche, the great philosopher, said 'We cannot get rid of God until we get rid of grammar.' Words are one of the greatest apologetics for the existence of God. God calls himself the Word in John 1.

My husband replied to her, 'What you're saying is this: words only have the meaning that the reader gives them. I'm the listener here, you've been talking. That means that I provide the interpretation. Is it OK then to take the words that you have just said to mean that "I'm a Christian and trusting in Jesus Christ for my salvation? Is that all right with you?"' She said 'No!' Suddenly the penny dropped. How can these post-modern writers tell us there is no God and that words have no meaning? They have to use words to do it. Yet this question of interpretation is raised again and again. Sometimes these intellectual questions are a smokescreen, an excuse not to be a Christian.

I'm a good person

In our post-modern culture, morality has become increasingly relativised. We cannot say that some things are right and some wrong. I was listening to *Question Time* recently and a moral question was raised and every single panellist was saying 'I couldn't make a moral question of that. I can't impose my morality on someone else.' This is a hallmark of post-modernism. There are no absolutes. Within that is the hope 'I'm a good person.'

Bertrand Russell, the great atheist, had a series of debates with a guy called Fredrick Copleston. As an atheist, Russell was trying to defend the idea that there was no God. Copleston was saying that if there was no God, how can there be any right or wrong? He asked Russell 'If you do not believe God as the lawgiver and there are no absolutes, how do you distinguish between good and evil?' Bertrand Russell said 'I distinguish between good and evil on the basis of how I feel.'[2] That is an intrinsically postmodern statement. Good and evil are about me and how I feel about the world. That's what happens when you remove God from the picture.

The atheist Richard Dawkins takes this one step further and writes 'In a universe of blind physical forces and genetic replication, some people are going to get hurt, other people are going to get lucky and you won't find any rhyme or reason in it nor any justice. The universe we observe has precisely the properties we should expect if there is at the bottom no design, no purpose, no evil and no good. Nothing but blind pitiless indifference. DNA neither knows nor cares, DNA just is and we dance to its music.'[3]

One of my friends once asked Richard Dawkins, 'You say there is no good or evil and no absolute terms; what about the holocaust? Would you say that was evil?' He said 'No. I can say I don't like it. But I can't say it was evil.'

The existence of evil in the world brings God's existence into question. It's a wonderful opportunity: if you dispense with God, who is the judge? It is God who gives the moral law of the universe. He provides us with absolutes that apply wherever we live in the universe.

Remember what Peter says to you. Don't be intimidated by long words. Peter is saying simply 'Have conversations, talk to people, live a Christian life that will call forth questions from others and when you get the opportunities, be ready. Get fit, put the work in, find out the questions that your friends have and find out the answers.'

We live in a post-modern culture where there is confusion, disillusionment and cynicism about truth. This is the context into which we are called to preach Christ and him crucified. Damien Hirst, the famous artist and also a postmodern thinker, said 'Nothing is important; everything is . . . I don't know why I'm here, but I'm glad I am – I'd rather be here than not . . . I am going to die and I want to live for ever. I can't escape the fact, and I can't let go of the desire.'[4]

This is the heart cry of our generation and we have the answer in the person and work of Christ. Let's learn from the model of Jesus, let's fall into conversation with people. Let's ask them questions, let's be ready and prepared.

Endnotes

[1] Quote from the *Sunday Times* magazine, 25th September 1999.

[2] Bertrand Russell, *Why I am not a Christian* (London: Routledge, 1992).

[3] Richard Dawkins: *River Out of Eden: A Darwinian View of Life* (Phoenix Press: 1996).

[4] Quoted on the following website:
    http://www.mfah.org/exhibition.asp?par1=1&par2=1&par3=366&par4=1&par5=1&par6=1&par7=&lgc=4&eid=&currentPage=

The Seminar

The era of the evangelist

by Luis Palau

Luis Palau

Luis Palau was born and raised in an affluent family in Argentina, and discovered Christ while a child. Shortly after receiving his doctorate from Multnomah Biblical Seminary in Portland, Oregon, he returned to Latin America, building an evangelistic team and helping other evangelists – including interpreting for Billy Graham, a primary influence on Luis's own ministry. By the early 1980s, Luis Palau's ministry had made a great impact in western Europe and new doors were opening around the globe. With his sons, Luis now runs a successful festival evangelism ministry.

The era of the evangelist: Part 1

Who are evangelists?

When you think about evangelism, the Scripture gives us several pictures. For a start, we are ambassadors for Christ, as though God were speaking through us. To me, it is a fascinating thing that we should see ourselves as ambassadors. When I think of an ambassador, I think of dignity, honour, propriety, a sense of authority. I have met a few ambassadors here and there and they are always well-dressed, always ready for a TV interview, ready all the time. They also have a message not made by themselves but delegated by their government, usually the president or the prime minister. Ambassadors don't tell the other governments whatever crosses their minds. They deliver a message that has been given to them but they don't create it. So when you think about sharing the faith, think of yourself – I have dignity, I have authority, I have a message, I have grandeur – not in myself but because of whom I represent. You are not alone – you have the full authority and power of the Commander in Chief, the King of Kings, and the Lord of Lords. Doesn't that do something for you?

Fishermen

Fishermen are fanatics. I know because one of our sons is a fisherman and he is a fanatic. Andrew loves to fish. He has one clear mind, he is very focused – nothing is as important as catching fish. Fishermen

Luis Palau

love to fish and when the Lord said I will make you fishers of men, he was speaking about focus – the goal of a fisherman is to catch fish and the goal of a spiritual fisherman is to catch souls. We should be unashamed of it. I'm a net fisherman – I love lots of fish in one shot!

Witnesses

What is a witness? A witness is a person of character – you have to have character so you can be believed – but you also have to be a person of words. You cannot be a witness with your mouth shut. Suppose you go to court, as a witness, and the judge says to you, 'Mr. Palau, what did you see at 3pm at the corner of such and such when an accident took place?' If you then do what many of us do spiritually, you would say, 'Judge, I will say not a word. I want my life to speak for itself.' The judge would probably say 'Mr. Palau, you tell us what you saw or you will go to jail. You cannot just sit there and say I want to let my life speak for itself. Yes, your life should back you up. You haven't evangelized unless you have opened your mouth. It is good and wonderful to say my life is godly but eventually you have to speak, otherwise the good news isn't the good news. It seems basic but it is amazing how many people get confused on that issue.

A witness has to say two things – what you have seen and what you have heard. It is always good to remember that when the apostle Paul was in a pinch, he told his story over and over again. In the book of Acts the story is told three times. In the epistles, he mentions snatches of it. You can do the same – tell your story, how you came to know the Lord Jesus Christ, who helped you. It is amazing how the Holy Spirit opens up when you do so, even if the story isn't very dramatic.

My story is very bland – I came to the Lord at twelve years old, at a summer camp. I went to Sunday School, I had never beaten up my mother-in-law because I didn't have one: I had never done drugs because there were no drugs in those days, I had never got drunk except once and I hated it – so I had no big sins to confess. So when I told my story, I was always afraid people were going to say 'There's nothing interesting here. But you would be amazed how many times, when I tell it, people will come up and say, 'I was touched by your story . . .' What was so touching about it? Except that the Lord Jesus Christ came into my life . . .

Farmers

Farmers in the Bible do two things – sowing and reaping. You sow the seed of God, the word of God – you plant biblical messages, biblical passages in people's minds. The older I'm getting, the more Bible verses I tend to quote when I am preaching the gospel because the Bible has power in itself, just like a seed. The more you plant that, the more fruit you will be able to see.

The farmer plants the seed and then you have to wait for a period of time – the rain has to come, the sun has to shine – later in the year the harvest comes through. It is the same thing from a spiritual point of view – you sow the seed and you would love somebody to be converted on the spot and from time to time it happens, in the Lord's goodness, but a lot of time you plant seeds and it takes years. Be patient and don't despair: plant the seed, water it if you can, and the Lord will make the sun shine on it and eventually it will come to fruition. And the second thing farmers do is reap. Suddenly it is harvest time and a lot of people come in.

Evangelizing and witnessing isn't easy in our secular world. But on the other hand it is not as hard as sometimes we think it is, if we are willing to go out on a limb and obey the Holy Spirit. Evangelism actually is praise to God – sharing the good news – it isn't just a chore that you are accomplishing. It isn't just a duty you are performing, though it is a duty – we don't always feel like it, we don't always have fun doing it, though sometimes we do – but actually you do it because the Master says do it. One of the great things about evangelism is that so often we immediately think in terms of methodology. Now methodology is important but it isn't the first thing that should grip us when we think of evangelism. The Bible doesn't tell us what way to do evangelism. It gives us the message, the message is sacred, but the methods are not. It just tells us, do it!

Part 2: The battle for souls

Every believer is a witness but not every believer has the gift of being an evangelist – thank the Lord for that. Imagine if all of us were evangelists, what a mess it would be: we would all be preaching at each other and nobody would be listening! I have travelled to many countries and what always amazes me is how many humble people, with minimal education, are active in sharing their faith. You would be amazed at what insight they have into the good things we have in Jesus Christ.

A passion for souls

How do you get a love for the lost? How do you get a passion for souls? That phrase is old-fashioned and some young people say 'We love people, not souls.' But it is a soul that makes a person. When you say 'a passion for souls', it is because you are thinking of the eternal dimension as well.

R.A. Torrey was an associate of Dwight Moody, who was an evangelist who loved the UK. He said there were three things you had to do: the first was to read what the Scripture says about the present state and future destiny of those who are without Christ: secondly, you have to believe what the Scripture says about the present state and future destiny of those who are without Christ, and finally, you have to begin to pray on the basis of what the Bible says about the present state and destiny of those who are without Christ.

It takes time in God's holy word to figure out what is the present state of those without Jesus Christ and when you begin to meditate on it and believe it, you get on your knees and say, 'Lord, the present state of those without Christ is that they are in darkness, they are lost, they have no hope, they don't have the Holy Spirit, they are not children of God, they are searching like blind people looking for the door and they can't find it, they are dead spiritually – Lord, help me to bring them to yourself.'

Then you think about the eternal state of those who die without Christ, and you take it to heart and get on your knees and listen to the word of the Lord and say 'God, I have got to do something, it is not right, it is awful how people are living.' You don't tell people everything you know but you do present to them the good news of Jesus Christ and when you do that, you do it counting on the Holy Spirit, depending on him.

Throughout history there have been some men and women whom we have called outstanding special people of God – who have led people to Christ – Martin Luther, John Wesley, George Whitfield, Finney, Moody, Spurgeon, Billy Sunday, Corrie ten Boom, Billy Graham . . . what did they have that made them so powerful that we remember them hundreds of years later?

What do you need to do?

I have always believed that if you want to be an evangelist, there are three basic things you need to do. You must be a man or a woman of the word – you have got to know the Bible and the more you know it, the better. Yes, you can tell stories and give illustrations, but it has got to be grounded in the Bible. Secondly, you need to know your history: history is vital because it keeps you in balance. An evangelist ought to know church history because not only does it give you the broad picture but also it keeps you from repeating the same foolish things that others have done – we learn from their mistakes. And thirdly, you need to read biography. I have been so blessed by Christian biography, the good kind, the serious kind.

What do you need to be?

All these people I have mentioned had some characteristics in common. Firstly, they were men or women of fire, the fire of the Holy Spirit – we can have it if we believe he is there and we let him speak through us. There is a difference between the fire of the Holy Spirit and the fire of the flesh. When we are young and we are starting out, we can imitate other people – I know I did! The fire of the Spirit is not related to outward trappings: the power comes from the Spirit of God.

Then, they were men and women of holy audacity. When you look at Luther, Calvin, even Billy Graham, they all used audacious methods. They are always at the vanguard of changing things. Methods change – don't fight about methods, as long as they are ethical – are they communicating the gospel of Jesus Christ? These men and women had great audacity and they would do anything to communicate the gospel.

They were also men and women of a national vision. Start where you are and do what you can. You will sweat like crazy but rely on the Holy Spirit, and you will have the right answers at the right time. You don't have to know all the answers – you're not God. One of the best answers is 'I don't know.'

Not only that, but a true person who has a love for souls cares for the whole world: it is a natural outcome because the Holy Spirit gives you a love for the world. I always like to recommend that if the Lord lays a certain country on your heart, even if you may never go there, take it upon yourself to pray for that country, get a map of that country, pray for the cities, make it part of your life in the Spirit, because things happen in the world of the Spirit through prayer and intercession that not everybody can understand. There is a power when there is prayer that we cannot explain. Prayer and intercession carry power and one grows in prayer and intercession. At first it seems like a big chore to pray for five minutes but then you begin to grow.

People talk a lot about spiritual warfare. If you want to get into spiritual warfare, start evangelizing and the war will come to you. If you use methods that are new, someone is going to get upset. They will say anything to upset you and try to shut you up. People used to attack Billy Graham . . . if you are sharing the good news, be ready. A little opposition stimulates my spiritual adrenalin – it is healthy and it gets the best out of you.

These people were also clearly free from the love of money – they didn't let money stick to their fingers. Some people have an excessive love for money and they often misuse it. They also had a great love for the whole body of Christ. We have differences about music, serving communion, baptism – and these things are important – but they are not basic. Normal people disagree on details – otherwise we would all be so boring! And finally, these men and women were greatly local church-centred – they loved the churches. An evangelist has to love the local church!

Part 3: A heart for the world

It is often easier to evangelise when you go somewhere else than it is to evangelise in your own town. It is much easier to go to India – it takes less courage to witness there then to witness in your home town, because no one knows you there. In a stadium, it is easy to preach – there are a hundred thousand people, they are thirty yards away from you, you can shout at them. But if you have thirty-five people at a tea in Keswick, it is a different story. You look at them, you wonder what they are thinking, you pray: 'Lord, you've got to help me here. These people never respond, they never smile, they don't even bat an eyelid, and I don't even know if they are listening!' Finally you get a little reaction and you say, 'Thank the Lord!'

God has given us power: you don't have to have the gift of evangelism. He has given us the Holy Spirit, and the Holy Spirit indwells us all. Quote the Bible . . . what is there to lose?

How to encourage an evangelist

If there is someone in your church who says they have the gift of evangelism, encourage them. Pray for them. Spend time with them. Those who have the gift of evangelism have a certain temperamental inclination. I have been around them, I happen to be one – they tend to be a bit more exuberant, a bit more outgoing, a bit bolder. Inside – I know, I deal with hundreds of them – they have strengths and weaknesses. Their strengths need to be encouraged but their weaknesses need to be dealt with. Evangelists don't like to be told anything: they feel they know pretty much everything. There is a bit of a problem there but if you love them and help them with a few pounds once in a while, they will listen to you. They need adult men and women who will stand by them and stand up to them when they say foolish things.

What are evangelists?

Evangelists and those who share the good news are, in a sense, leaders. It says in Ephesians that God gave leadership gifts: apostles, prophets, evangelists, pastors and teachers. Evangelists can lead by helping people's faith and they ought to be given that chance. Ministers are more shepherds, more patient people – like fathers. Evangelists have that strength, that they do believe God, that he has power, that he hasn't lost his enthusiasm for the great commission, and they have a tendency to remind the body of Christ that God hasn't lost his enthusiasm for it.

Evangelists are also people of courage and selfless abandon: they have a tendency to go for broke and to do extreme things. And sometimes for that they are criticized. Whenever you go out and proclaim the good news, you have got to be ready for criticism, and sometimes persecution and even danger. Evangelists have courage and you have to encourage that.

If an evangelist comes to your town, the first thing you should ask is 'Are they backed up by their local church? Do they attend there or do they think they are above the church?' I wouldn't accept any evangelist who thinks they are above the local church. The other thing is that evangelists have a tendency to get angry if the local church doesn't support them, and they get critical of the church. We have to tell them to stop attacking the church, and to do their job and to let the pastors do theirs. Evangelists need to be reminded to respect the local church, to love the local church, to be part of the local church. Bless them but be kindly bold with them. Prove your love.

People of vision

An evangelist is a person of vision who stirs vision in the body of Christ. This should be encouraged, not just for the young people, but for the middle aged and older people too. It is so good to see retired people who are fired up, who have a youthful spirit. Every town should have a united mission at least every ten years, when the whole town comes together. Evangelists also tend to embrace the whole body of Christ and to ignore secondary differences: to bring the whole body together to confront a world that is lost for eternity. An evangelist, if they are walking in the Spirit, will unite the body of Christ and insist on the unity of the Body of Christ. You can never get 100 per cent unity and there is always some recalcitrant local church that will not cooperate but you have got to go for the most and work together. The young people love it, the newspapers pay attention when you work together, the politicians perk up their ears. Even Jesus likes it, as it says in John 17: 'Father, may they be one as we are one, so the world may know that you sent me.' Insist on the unity of the body. They won't all be converted but they will all listen. Shake the town, wake them up. It is good for a city to be shaken.

An evangelist as a leader is someone who is worth imitating. The apostle Paul quite openly and shamelessly said, 'Be imitators of me as I am of Jesus Christ.' That is quite a statement, isn't it? Three times in the New Testament he said, 'Follow me as I follow Christ.' An evangelist ought to be able to say that, not because he is perfect, but because he so walks with Christ.

As British people, encourage evangelists and do your part, wherever you can, volunteer, be part of it, encourage these men and women who love the Lord, and go all out, give yourself 100 per cent. We have one chance in this world to evangelise, we don't know when the Lord is going to return. Evangelism is about honouring Jesus Christ; God loves to hear men speak well of his Son — even if no one is converted. That is what evangelism is, so give it all you've got. As long as I am alive, I want to speak well of his Son. And never, ever, give up.

The Addresses

A church just like mine?
1 Corinthians

Marriage: God's idea

by Alex Ross

Alex Ross is vicar of St James's, Muswell Hill, North London. He's worked for the Church of England for over thirty years in different churches. He has a great love for the local church because he believes it's God's way to save the world. The motto of St James's is *Loving Jesus and making him known*. He is married to Lynne and has three children.

Marriage: God's idea

1 Corinthians 7:1-16

Introduction

Corinth was like many of the other cities in Western Europe. It was a big, cosmopolitan, commercial city that indulged in all sorts of pleasure. I suppose that this is why the first letter to the Corinthians is such a relevant letter for us today, particularly chapter 7. It covers three main subjects in its first sixteen verses: marriage, singleness and sex.

Sex was a big issue for the Corinthian church. Chapter 5 talks about a man moving in with his step-mother, chapter 6 talks about picking up prostitutes and in chapter 7 Paul is talking about sex, marriage and singleness: issues being raised by the church (v1): 'Now for the matters you wrote about . . .' Paul is dealing with questions the church has raised. This is practical, down to earth stuff.

Corinth was called the Vanity Fair of the first century. There was a huge temple dominated by worship of Aphrodite, the Greek goddess of love. Historians tell us that there were a thousand priestesses in the temple who acted as prostitutes. It was a cult dedicated to the glorification of sex. This seemed to have affected the whole atmosphere of Corinth, so you can see why there were questions.

Sex is becoming an increasing feature of our culture. Many of us see the dramatic changes that have taken place over the last forty years.

We are now exposed to all sorts of explicit sexual behaviour. I don't know the statistics for our country but on American television 70 per cent of sexual activity is outside of marriage. Let's unpack this and apply it to our situation. Not that Paul is giving a comprehensive definition of marriage, sex or singleness. He's dealing with specific issues in Corinth. If you want a full definition, you'll have to look at the whole of the Bible.

There seemed to have been two different types of wrong perceptions in Corinth. There were the rigorists, who acted strongly against the sexual permissiveness of Corinth and had swung the opposite way. They were forbidding what God had created for us to enjoy. That is why Paul is saying that marriage and sex are gifts from God. Singleness is also a gift from God. Others on the other side of the pendulum were into freedom; saying that all things are now possible, in marriage and outside of marriage.

Marriage

Verse 2: 'But since there is so much immorality, each man should have his own wife, and each woman her own husband.' Paul knew what Corinth and the Christians were like and said that if you are being tempted sexually it's better to get married. Sex throughout the Bible is seen as God's wedding present, something to be enjoyed in marriage. This is why we have a high view of sex; it's God-given and we have to deal with it with dignity. Prostitution trivialises sex, affairs trivialise and demean sex. Having sexual intercourse is the most intimate experience that a man and woman can have together. That's why Paul repeats himself in verse 9: 'if they cannot control themselves, they should marry, for it is better to marry than to burn with passion.'

Paul knows that the suppression of sexual desires doesn't work, although he does have his critics at this point. They say he is belittling marriage; that just because you can't control yourself sexually is not a good enough reason to get married. But when you read the Bible, what are the grounds for marriage? As far as I can see there are only two. The first is that you have to have a man and a woman: the other is that you have to be covenant people: Jews in the Old Testament, Christians in the New. There is a lot of teaching about how husband and wife should live together, serve and sacrifice for each other, but there is nothing about marrying the right person, about being in love, even about being suitable and compatible. It may be wise to look at these things but they are not fundamental principles. There is no teaching that you marry the person of your dreams.

I remember talking to a friend of mine just a week before he got married. He had been engaged for a while and was quite mature. But he was dithering as to whether he was marrying the right woman. They seemed eminently suitable but he wasn't sure. So I talked to him about these two principles. I said you're a man and she's a woman; you're a Christian and she is a Christian, so there is no reason why you shouldn't get married. They got married, and as far as I can see they are very happy. Paul is not belittling marriage but giving a very down-to-earth common sense approach. If they can't control themselves, they should marry.

It is possible for us to get too spiritual and too intense. Paul's concern here is personal purity, morality and holiness. These are the things that really matter for us as Christians. Martin Luther was a great Christian leader and often had a very picturesque way of talking. Once when he was talking about marriage and sexual immorality, he said 'You can't stop the birds from flying overhead but you can stop them from nesting in your hair.' This is what Paul is saying. We can't stop having a sexual drive but through marriage we can stop immoral sexual behaviour. Holiness is a priority, morality is important.

Then, Paul says, once you are married, stay married. He says that four times: 'A wife must not separate from her husband' (v10), 'a husband must not divorce his wife' (v11), 'if any brother has a wife who is not a believer and she is willing to live with him he must not divorce her. And if a woman has a husband who is not a believer and he is willing to live with her, she must not divorce him' (vs 12,13) and 'if the unbeliever leaves, let him do so' (v15). Christian marriage is meant to be a life sentence – for richer, for poorer; for better, for worse; in sickness and in health, till death us do part. For many of us, it is worse, for many reasons. The verses are clear: get married and don't burn. Get married and stay married.

Sex

Paul shows that just because we are married this doesn't solve all our sexual problems. Sex can still be used for personal gratification (vs 3,5). It was probably particularly likely in a place like Corinth where sex was so easily available, where there were many prostitutes and you could pay your money and help yourself. Paul says it shouldn't be like that in marriage (vs 3-4): 'The husband should fulfil his marital duty to his wife, and likewise the wife to her husband. The wife's body does not belong to her alone but also to her husband. In the same way, the husband's body does not belong to him alone but also to his wife.' Notice how equally balanced it is between men and women; both sexes are to look out for each others' needs.

Herman Oestler, the German writer, said 'If you want to be happy, don't get married. You get married to make your partner happy.' It's so true with sex. Paul is touching a difficult area here because in some marriages there are real tensions over sex. People have very different sexual appetites. Some enjoy sex once a night, some once a year, but you'd expect that. Just look at how our appetites vary for food. We're all different shapes and sizes and have different capacities for food.

I was at a three year old's birthday party a little while ago and when it came to tea, one of the little boys became very serious and he just ate and ate and ate. At the end of meal he was surrounded by empty plates. He must have cost his parents hundred of pounds a week to keep! It is the same in marriage. Sexual desire varies enormously. How do we resolve it? Verse 3: each partner has a duty to the other. It doesn't sound very romantic, but we each have a commitment, a responsibility, an obligation. But what happens if our needs are different? Verse 4: her needs have to become his needs and his needs have to become her needs. My concern in marriage is not what I want but what my partner wants.

The Roman Catholic Church linked sexual intercourse primarily with having children. Interestingly, Paul doesn't restrict it in that way. He encourages us to have a regular and enthusiastic sex life but he does give a reason for denial; 'Do not deprive each other except by mutual consent and for a time, so that you may devote yourselves to prayer. Then come together again so that Satan may not tempt you because of your lack of self control' (v5). The only reason for replacing sexual intercourse is so that we can have a higher intercourse with God through prayer. This has to be done mutually.

Some enthusiastic Christians have got carried away by this. Going back to the Middle Ages, there was a Christian leader in Chartres in France who said: 'The devout are to abstain from sexual intercourse on Thursdays in remembrance of Christ's rapture . . . on Fridays in remembrance of Christ's crucifixion . . . on Saturdays in honour of the Virgin Mary . . . on Sunday in commemoration of Christ's resurrection (and) . . . on Mondays out of reverence for departed souls.' I imagine that the devout really looked forward to Tuesdays and Wednesdays! That wasn't in Paul's mind as he wrote this, but he is giving us practical principles for married people. I am responsible for the lifelong sexual satisfaction of my partner. To neglect sex in marriage is to cheat my partner. Paul is saying no sex without marriage and no marriage without sex.

Why does he say all this? He knows that sex is powerful. Sex outside marriage damages the Christian. He's already said this

> Flee from sexual immorality. All other sins a man commits are outside his body, but he who sins sexually sins against his own body. Do you not know that your body is a temple of the Holy Spirit, who is in you, whom you have received from God? You are not your own; you were bought at a price. Therefore honour God with your body (1 Cor. 6:18-19).

These are two massive motives for personal purity. We have been bought with the blood of Jesus and we are a temple of the Holy Spirit. Can you see two higher motives for holiness than those two? We are holy because of the blood of Christ; we are holy because of the Holy Spirit. It is only because Christ has sent us a power in our lives that we can begin to act out 1 Corinthians 7. Notice the priority is holiness, purity. So is sex for everyone? No.

Singleness

Paul starts this subject off at the very beginning of the chapter, (v1): 'It is good for a man not to marry.' At the footnote in the NIV we see that it says 'It is good for a man not to have sexual relations with a woman.' You can understand why Paul is making this statement in sex-mad Corinth. Everyone was doing it, and it can feel like that today. If we're not in a sexual relationship, we can feel left out, so it is good to remind ourselves of verse 1.

Later in the chapter he gives reasons why. To the single, he says (v26): 'Because of the present crisis, I think it is good for you to remain as you are.' Verse 28: 'those who marry will face many troubles in this life, and I want to spare you this.' Verses 32-34

> An unmarried man is concerned about the Lord's affairs – how he can please the Lord. But a married man is concerned about the affairs of this world – how he can please his wife – and his interests are divided. An unmarried woman or virgin is concerned about the Lord's affairs: Her aim is to be devoted to the Lord in both body and spirit. But a married woman is concerned about the affairs of this world – how she can please her husband.

Paul gives a very strong reason for why we shouldn't get married: it is for our holiness, so that we can set apart and serve the Lord. But how can we live like this?

Verse 7: 'I wish that all men were as I am. But each man has his own gift from God.' Paul is saying that the single life is a gift from God. This is important: otherwise we might try and be something that we are not. Asceticism has crept into Christianity throughout history. Some people have reacted to the sex-mad culture by deciding to withdraw and deny themselves pleasure. This is not just confined to Christianity. Muslims abstain during Ramadan; Buddhist monks and Hindu holy men abstain. We have the equivalent in Christianity with monks, nuns and Roman Catholic priests. Is this what Paul is advocating? Not really. He's not asking for denial of physical pleasure. He's not asking for a denial of physical enjoyment. Listen to what he says in Colossians: 'Such regulations have an appearance of wisdom with the harsh treatment of the body but they lack any value in restraining sexual indulgence.'

Jerome was a fourth century monk, living in a sex-mad place, so he decided to move into the desert to try and deal with the problem. He wrote: 'Though in my fear of hell I'd consigned myself to this prison where my only companions were scorpions and wild beasts, I often found myself amid bevies of girls. My face was pale and my frame chilled with fasting, yet my mind was inflamed with desire.' Even though he went away from all the distractions of life, he still had this great sexual urge. This is why Paul is saying that singleness is a gift from God, and we either have this gift or we don't.

Some people think that if you are single you are a second class citizen, you are left unfulfilled. Paul certainly hints that he was single in verse 7. Was Paul unfulfilled? Jesus was a single man. Do you think Jesus was unfulfilled? Over the years there have been some single men who have had a major influence in my life and I would never dream that they were unfulfilled. They were set apart for God's service. Not that the single life is without pain, not that the single life doesn't leave people with an ache and a longing. But if we have this gift, God says it is good not to marry.

The church has not always been helpful because it has moved away from the Bible on some of these issues. Gregory of Nyssa was a fourth century bishop. He describes marriage as a sad tragedy. Paul calls it a gift from God. Paul says get married and stay married. Tertullian, a second century theologian, said that the difference between sex inside and outside of marriage is only a matter of legal small print. Paul says sex is God's wedding present for marriage. It is to be enjoyed within marriage. Some Christians think that singleness is a second rate life. Paul says that singleness is the best way to live if you have that gift because you are set free to serve Christ more fully. But all this teaching is for a higher priority, to live as God's people, to live for the Lord's glory.

Maybe some of you are wondering about marriage or wondering whether you have the gift of singleness; maybe you are struggling to work out whether singleness is something that God has given you.

These are real issues. These are in the Bible: practical everyday issues that we need to face up to. What has God got to say to us? They are written here for our holiness so that we can live for Christ in a whole-hearted and clear way.

Free to serve

by Peter Lewis

Peter Lewis

Peter Lewis is the senior minister of the Cornerstone Evangelical Church, Nottingham, where he has served with his wife Valerie for 37 years. The church has grown in that time from forty to fifty adults to over six hundred, plus about 180 children. It has a strong emphasis on Bible-teaching, evangelism and cross-cultural mission. A large team of full-time and part-time church workers unite in leading various aspects of the church's work, from refugee work to youth ministry. Peter is also the author of *The Glory of Christ, The Message of the Living God* and *God's Hall of Fame*. He and Valerie have two sons, Calvin and Justin.

Free to serve

I Corinthians 9:19-23

Introduction

Our overall theme this week is the church in the power of the Spirit. In our chapter this evening, we'll see this major lesson: that an important ingredient in Christian power is a certain type of weakness. It's a voluntary weakness, modelled on the weakness of the incarnate Christ.

At the heart of Christian truth is the servant King, who did not count equality with God something to be used for his advantage but for ours. He had everything but made himself nothing. And on the cross of Calvary, he made himself less than nothing as he took upon himself personal responsibility for the world's cruelty, sin and rebellion against God. Yet the weakness of God proved stronger than man's strength, as the resurrection of Jesus Christ showed. He lifted our burdens, even as he himself was crushed under them. He opened heaven to us, even as he himself entered hell for us, on the cross at Calvary. In giving up his rights, he established our own.

Paul's concern is that all Gospel ministry, and indeed all Christian life and witness, should reflect this and act out its principle of love and self giving. Virtually every chapter of 1 Corinthians, from 8 to 14, illustrates this, as he answers the questions raised by this Corinthian church, with all its self assertion and division. Chapter 9 isn't a digression but a part of the on-going argument with this troublesome people at Corinth. In it he shows how, when he first came to Corinth, Paul carefully subordinated his rights to the good of others.

Giving up his rights

Evidence in the book of Acts and the letters to the Corinthians suggest that, throughout his time there, Paul stayed in the home of Aquila and Priscilla. They had been expelled from Rome, with other Jews, by the emperor Claudius. They'd come to Corinth, famous for its prosperity and its trade, and set up their small shop to sell leather goods and tents. You can still see such shops in the ruins of old Corinth. They weren't large; perhaps about thirteen feet by thirteen feet by eight feet high. Possibly Aquila and Priscilla made their home in the loft above the shop, while Paul slept below, amid the tool strewn work benches and rolls of leather and canvas. The workshop was perfect for initial contacts, particularly with women. While Paul worked on a cloak or sandal or belt, he had the opportunity for conversation which quickly became instruction and further encounters would be easily justified by the need for other repairs.

The idea of Paul working long hard hours, in the broiling heat of Corinth, might impress us but it didn't impress the Corinthians. They didn't like this business and this visibility at all. The *nouveau riche* of that booming city had appearances to keep up. One of the important aspects of Corinthian social life was its cultural life, and one of the features of that were the sophists, with their public lectures in philosophy and their impressive displays of rhetoric. Rhetoric was and is a way of structuring an argument so as to attract and convince an audience. It had an illustrious place and history in the Greek and Roman world. Rhetoric was famously exemplified by the Roman Cicero and, centuries before, the Greek Demosthenes. As a way of presenting a good cause, it was honourable and sometimes necessary in public speaking.

Paul himself could argue his case this way and was no mean rhetorician but rhetoric could easily be abused and degenerate into an entertainment, an art form. The sophists specialised in it and they travelled around the ancient Roman world, as expert performers and talkers, rather like the chat show hosts or media figures of the present day. They made a good living out of it; charging fees and staying in a city, usually under the patronage of a well-off member of that particular society.

Many of the new Christians at Corinth would have liked Paul to turn professional and to be like the sophists. He was their man, part of their image. The sight of their chosen teacher continuing to work, throughout this time, in a common trade where everybody could see him, became frankly embarrassing. In a city where social climbing was a major occupation, Paul's deliberate stepping down in apparent status would have been seen by many of them as disturbing, disgusting and even provocative.

What a challenge, in standards and values, enters our lives when we become Christians; when we have to approve ourselves to God and not to human beings. Even as Christians, we can find it all too easy to seek the approval of our peers rather than our Lord. It's a lesson they had to learn, it's a lesson we all have to learn. Especially, perhaps, people who stand on platforms at conventions like this.

Many who look after aged and invalided relatives, many of our international workers who serve God in out-of-the-way places, in obscure causes or in far-flung mission stations, wash feet for Christ, in a room where nobody sees and nobody knows. The model of servanthood is the Christ who not only washed feet but went on to wash souls by his atoning death. When Paul went to Corinth, his first concern was to preach a crucified Christ, and to preach it, he had to live it. He distanced himself from the sophists and the rhetoricians, from the start, even in his lifestyle and determinedly, publicly, pointedly, lived by his hands, working at the family trade.

The Greeks tended to look down on manual labour. But to the Jews, it was part of God's creation order and had always had its own dignity. Even the Rabbis had a trade. Paul seems to have come from a well-to-do business family in Tarsus, and learnt the family trade. Paul himself is no mean rhetorician, and he now deals with this matter in an expert and unanswerable way.

What were Paul's rights?

First, he demonstrates his rights. Then he shows his right to set aside his rights. Verse 1: 'Am I not free? Am I not an apostle? Have I not seen Jesus our Lord? Are you not the result of my work in the Lord? Even though I may not be an apostle to others, surely I am to you! For you are the seal of my apostleship in the Lord.'

Paul is going to show that he is entitled to their financial and other support on many grounds. As Christians they have a high view of the apostles of Jesus. Let them remember that he too is an apostle, commissioned by the risen Christ and equal in apostolic status and authority to any of the original disciples. They themselves are a result of that and a seal on his apostleship. But they, with all their airs and graces, are only Christians because a preacher came to Corinth, in weakness, fear and much trembling, and preached a crucified Christ, in the power of the Spirit of God. Then let them see the inconsistency of their position and its vanities. Paul's argument is, 'You yourselves are proof of what *I'm* saying and a contradiction of what *you're* saying. This is my defence to those who sit in judgement on me.'

In verses 7 to 12, he shows that he had every right to live by their support, as much as any farmer has a right to eat from his own harvest. And yet, in verse 12, he says, 'we did not use this right. On the contrary, we put up with anything, rather than hinder the gospel of Christ.' In the particular context of Corinth, Paul had been led to adopt a particular lifestyle. He was determined not to be put down as another travelling philosopher, giving performances to admiring audiences. He had rights even from God, (vs 14,15), 'In the same way, the Lord has commanded that those who preach the gospel should receive their living from the gospel. But I have not used any of these rights' – that is, in Corinth.

There's a further factor in this which we might easily miss. Travelling teachers, like the sophists and rhetoricians, had well-to-do patrons in the various cities and that patronage insured their comforts but it came with obligations. Paul realised that such indebtedness, to any group or individual, could compromise his position as an impartial apostle. He was the servant of all, not just of people of influence. There were others at Corinth who weren't so scrupulous. That's why Paul says, in his second letter, that he had been willing to receive and accept the gifts of the Philippians when he left Macedonia, up north, but wasn't willing to be supported by the Corinthians, in this wealthy city, with its conditions and expectations, either then or later. Verse 15-18

> But I have not used any of these rights. And I am not writing this in the hope that you will do such things for me. I would rather die than have anyone deprive me of this boast. Yet when I preach the gospel, I cannot boast, for I am compelled to preach. Woe to me if I do not preach the gospel! If I preach voluntarily, I have a reward; if not voluntarily, I am simply discharging the trust committed to me. What then is my reward? Just this: that in preaching the gospel I may offer it free of charge, and so not make use of my rights in preaching it.

What that boils down to is this: he can't expect payment of any sort for doing what he must do anyway, that is preach the gospel. But he can do one thing which goes beyond that and receives its own reward. His reward is the privilege and joy of preaching the good news free of charge, offering the gospel without strings attached, in a culture where there were many strings attached to many gods.

Making himself a slave

Then we come to this great passage, (vs 19-23)

> Though I am free and belong to no man, I make myself a slave to everyone, to win as many as possible. To the Jews I became like a Jew, to win the Jews. To those under the law I became like one under the law (though I myself am not under the law), so as to win those under the law. To those not having the law I became like one not having the law (though I am not free from God's law but am under Christ's law), so as to win those not having the law. To the weak I became weak, to win the weak. I have become all things to all men so that by all possible means I might save some. I do all this for the sake of the gospel, that I may share in its blessings.

As Paul travelled from city to city, preaching the gospel to the Jew first and also to the Greek, starting with the synagogue and going out into the market place, there was a consistent inconsistency about his manner of life. Among Jews, he would keep the Jewish food laws and customs, out of respect for the group around him. Among Gentiles, he would exercise his freedom from such restrictions. He was no longer under the obligations of the old covenant, as he had been as a Pharisee. He was not under the law of Moses as a matter of principle. In Christ, he was in a position that transcended all cultural allegiances. But he was free to put himself under its restrictions, if it would help him reach his fellow Jews with the good news about Jesus the Messiah. Similarly, in the churches, he would accommodate himself to the needs of others. He would stand alongside the different groups, affirming their freedoms and protecting their interests, all the while restricting his own freedom for their good and teaching others to do so too.

Martin Luther famously articulates Paul's principle, in his work concerning Christian liberty, and he has this ringing sentence which is famous, 'A Christian is the most free lord of all and subject to none. A Christian is the most dutiful servant of all and subject to everyone.' An important ingredient, in the power of the Spirit, is weakness: this kind of weakness, from people with his kind of power.

To the Gentiles, those outside the law, Paul was as a Gentile, as one outside the law, that is in respect to the Jewish laws. He himself was not lawless but he was under the law of Christ. He now lives, not under the obligation of an old law, but in the power of a new relationship. And in a dramatic metaphor, in verse 19, he says, 'I make myself a slave to everyone', even and especially to the weak – that is, to the socially disadvantaged and the vulnerable and the marginalised.

All this was not only a controversial attitude among Jews but in other ways among Gentiles too. Taking a lower station or place in society was not seen as a virtue. It was seen as slavish behaviour, not the sort of thing to which the upwardly mobile would ever aspire. But, to Paul, this was the mark of Christian leadership. Some of his converts had an all-too-worldly vision of Christian leadership. Paul's is the vision of the servant King who came, not to be served but to serve and to give his life as a ransom for many. For Paul, sharing the sufferings of Christ included all this. He died daily, as he says elsewhere. Paul's life, as well as his preaching, was cruciform. It is a manner of life which astonishes the world but delights the Saviour.

Running the race

All that touches us and challenges us and it mustn't leave us unchanged. To be changed like this is not the work of a day but of long years; years of vision, worship and disciplined training. That's why we mustn't leave out of the picture what follows in verse 24. 'Do you not know that in a race all the runners run, but only one gets the prize? Run in such a way as to get the prize. Everyone who competes in the games goes into strict training. They do it to get a crown that will not last; but we do it to get a crown that will last forever.'

Corinth was famous for its games. They were second only to the Olympic games. The crown was given to the victor but it wasn't made of olive branches, as we often think, until the second century. In Paul's day, the crown was made of celery and it was already withered when it was placed on the head of the victor. It was a crown that didn't and couldn't last. Paul looked for a crown that will last forever.

Verse 26, 'Therefore I do not run like a man running aimlessly; I do not fight like a man beating the air. No, I beat my body and make it my slave so that after I have preached to others, I myself will not be disqualified for the prize.' Beating his body refers to his day to day discipline and self denial, not as an ascetic, not even as an athlete, but as an apostle. Throughout it all, his eye is on the final goal: the 'Well done, good and faithful servant of the Lord Jesus Christ.' Paul was running for the victor's crown.

The alternative possibility doesn't dominate him but it does spur him on. The alternative is not damnation but a kind of disqualification. In the games they were disqualified not only for cheating in the event, but for cheating in the long months of training running up to the event. Paul is determined that he will not be disqualified by breaking the rules of his training and his race, which are happening together.

Disqualification here, in Paul's meaning, is not the loss of his soul but the loss of the prize of the high calling he's received from Christ as an apostle; the kind of loss he described in chapter 3 as 'escaping from the flames': saved but as by fire. Paul is referring here to worldly ministries being burned up on the last day, leaving the person ashamed and only saved by the skin of their teeth. That's what he's looking at and he's determined it won't happen to him. He's determined he will not be disqualified for the prize of the high calling, for the 'Well done good and faithful servant' but he will be victorious.

He says, 'I do not run aimlessly.' That means running with an indistinct or an unclear goal, distracted and failing to keep one's eye clearly on the goal. Do you know the story of Atlanta and Hippomenes? Atlanta was the daughter of a king. She was beautiful and suitors were many. Atlanta was athletic and suitors were challenged to race for her hand in marriage. They were not to race against each other but against her. Atlanta was famously fast and she was also ruthless. If they won, they had her hand in marriage but if they lost, they forfeited their lives. Many ran, all lost and none survived the experience or lived to love again or more wisely.

The judge of all the races was a man called Hippomenes and eventually he too came under her spell and offered himself for the contest. But first, he obtained three golden apples from Aphrodite, the goddess of love. They shot from the starting line and skimmed over the sand. At first Hippomenes drew ahead but she soon gained on him. Then he threw one of the golden apples to one side. Intrigued and very confident, Atlanta diverted off the path to pick up the golden object, while he gained ground. Quickly, she resumed the race and again started to catch him up. Again he threw a golden apple, as far as he could, to one side. Again she hesitated and ran to pick it up, strangely intrigued by the exquisite object. A third time, he gained ground and as he raced for the finishing post, a third time she caught him up and started to pass him. Desperately, he threw his golden apple in front of her and to the side and, unable to resist and still confident, for the third time, Atlanta stopped to pick up a golden apple. But this time, not even she could make up the ground that remained. Hippomenes won both the race and Atlanta's hand in marriage.

Personally, I wouldn't have touched her with a barge pole. Some men like strong minded women!

Don't be distracted

My point in telling you this story is quite simply this; beware of the golden apples in life, the attractions that take you off course in your Christian race. The golden apples defeated Atlanta as they've defeated many. It may be a relationship that is not going to help you in your Christian course. It may be ambitions, to which Jesus Christ often takes second place in your life. For someone else, it may be sexual attractions that pull you off course again and again. For others, it may be materialism. The remedy is to fix your eyes on the goal, the prize of the high calling of Jesus Christ; the look at the last day, in the first five minutes after death; the amazing statement that you can hardly believe: 'Well done, good and faithful servant.' Fix your eyes on the goal, the prize, the calling and let your entire life be lived in sight and hearing of that.

Every gain in this world is temporal but the goal of Christ is eternal. Through eternal ages and a new heavens and a new earth, all is unfolding. Every failure and set back and loss in life is secondary to this but not the gaining of Christ in his fullness, which is supreme.

Some of you are near the end of a long race and the finishing tape is in sight. Stay on course. You've not gone this far to give up or to surrender to doubts and distractions. They always come thick and fast in your last years, because of natural weakness: and the devil's no gentleman. Be of Paul's mind and heart in all your service for Christ. As he writes elsewhere, in Philippians 3:14, 'I press on towards the goal, to win the prize for which God has called me heavenwards in Christ Jesus.'

I was reading, just before I came, of something Joni Eareckson Tada likes to talk about: the special Olympics. An incident happened. There was one race in which a Down's syndrome girl approached the finishing tape and noticed that one of her companions had suddenly been distracted and wandered away, completely off the course.

Everybody was shouting to him but he didn't take any notice. In the end, she was within a few yards of the finishing tape and stopped, turned round, ran off the track, got hold of him, dragged him back on and they ran through the tape arm in arm together. The entire stadium stood up and clapped.

You may think, 'Didn't she take her eye off the finishing tape? Wasn't she distracted from her race?' By worldly standards, she took her eyes off the finishing tape. By spiritual standards, she kept them right on the right finishing tape, when she went to collect her friend.

Your ambitions are one finishing tape, Christ's call may be another. It may be that just as you're breaking through into all the promise of the years, another finishing tape is inviting you to take a different direction, to come off one track, even a fast track and to get on to another and to race a marathon, at the end of which will be an old man or woman, who looks back on the celery crowns that their friends wore, won and lost and will say, 'I chose well. My crown, my treasure, is just on the other side of the next few months.'

**Lessons for today from
New Testament Churches**

Colossae

by Liam Goligher

Liam Goligher

Liam Goligher has been Senior Pastor of Duke Street Church in Richmond since April 2000. He has pastored churches in Ireland, Canada and in his native Scotland, and is a Trustee of Keswick Ministries. His teaching is heard weekly on Premier Radio, Sky Digital and Freeview. His Duke Street ministry is available online.

Liam has contributed to a number of books, as well as writing three of his own: *Window on Tomorrow, The Fellowship of the King* and *The Jesus Gospel*. He is married to Christine, whom he met when they were both studying at the Irish Baptist College in Belfast. They have five children, three grandchildren and a Bedlington Terrier!

Colossae

Introduction

Let's look at Colossians, chapter 1:15-20

> He is the image of the invisible God, the firstborn of all creation. For by him all things were created, in heaven and on earth, visible and invisible, whether thrones or dominions or rulers or authorities – all things were created through him and for him. And he is before all things, and in him all things hold together. And he is the head of the body, the church. He is the beginning, the firstborn from the dead, that in everything he might be pre-eminent. For in him all the fullness of God was pleased to dwell, and through him to reconcile to himself all things, whether on earth or in heaven, making peace by the blood of his cross.

Whenever you get a letter from an apostle, you sit up and take notice, because a letter from Paul is a word from God. If it's being read to you for the very first time, you'll be wondering, 'Why is he writing to us? What is it that's on his mind, as he writes?'

If you want to know the reason why he's writing this book, look at chapter 2:6-8. He wants them to continue in Christ. He's already said that, when he talks about them being strengthened with all might in their inner person, for all endurance. In chapter 2:6 he picks this theme up again and says, 'Therefore, as you received Christ Jesus the Lord, so walk in him, rooted and built up in him and established in the faith, just as you were taught, abounding in thanksgiving.' He's concerned that these Colossian Christians should continue in the relationship with Jesus in which they've began. And there's a connection he wants them to make between how they received the Lord Jesus and how they go on in him. He doesn't want their continuing in Christ to be disjointed from their initial relationship with Christ.

He goes on to explain in chapter 2:8 why he says this: because they were in danger of being taken captive through 'hollow and deceptive philosophies'. 'Don't let anyone persuade you that you need another way of thinking about the world or about God.' In verse 16, he says, 'Do not let anyone judge you by what you eat or drink.' 'Don't make anyone make you feel guilty.' In verse 18 he says, 'Do not let anyone who delights in false humility and the worship of angels disqualify you for the prize.' 'Don't let anyone write you off, in your Christian life for one reason or another.'

Are you satisfied?

These are the three things that Paul has in his mind: they were in danger of being taken captive, of people making them feel guilty and of people disqualifying them. Imagine what was going on in the church at Colossae. People were coming from the outside (as very often false teaching does) and asking: 'Are you satisfied with your Christian life? Are you as happy as you once were? Do you have a close relationship with the Lord Jesus?'

Ask any of those questions to a new or even an older Christian, anyone who's keen, and invariably the answer you'll get is, 'I'm not satisfied with my Christian life.' It is a sin to feel you are satisfied, so you've got to say, 'I don't feel as close to Jesus as I did when I first believed. I'm dissatisfied.' The very question creates a vacuum in the minds and hearts of people. It goes on all the time in Christian circles today. People raise the questions and make ordinary believers doubt their experience. They lose or question their confidence. This was happening here in Colossae, and these people were also offering alternatives. This is where the real danger lay.

An alternative philosophy (v8)

They were saying, 'You need to look at the world in a different way. You need a new perspective on the world, to learn from the society around you. You live in a Greek society where philosophy abounds. As Christians living in this context, you can learn from these philosophies. You can contextualise the Gospel much more efficiently and effectively, if you learn from the principles that are motivating people around you.'

That happens today as well. People say to Christians, 'You need to start thinking the way the world thinks. We live in a post-modern world, so you need to start re-imagining and re-expressing the Christian faith in post-modern terms.' People are not confident any longer about anything. They will not make assertions that something is right or wrong. Everything is a shade of grey. And if you're going to relate to post-modern times, then you must never make confident assertions. You must blend in with the spirit of the age.

More religion (v16)

Others were encouraging these Christians to think in terms of religion. 'Therefore do not let anyone judge you ... with regard to a religious festival, a New Moon celebration or a Sabbath day.' They were saying, 'You need more religion in the formal sense: a more rules-orientated focus. In our churches, it's all very *laissez-faire*, very undisciplined and what we need is more structure, more order, more ceremony, more religion.'

Mysticism (vs 8, 18)

Others were offering mysticism. In verse 8, they're insisting on asceticism, the worship of angels and so on. They were recommending some kind of mystical experience. The views that they were bringing were Greek views of god: all kinds of emanations went out from god and the further away from god these emanations got, the more they got closer to this world. That was the Greek view and then the Jews superimposed upon the Greek view the idea that these emanations were angels, and what you wanted was an experience of one of these mighty spiritual beings. On jaded, tired and rather bored Christians, the appeal of these false teachers, then and still today, makes its impact.

People who are most easily led astray by false theology, false doctrine and ideas that don't come out of the Bible are bored Christians looking for something new. And what does it do, this new thing? Verse 18, 'It puffs up.'

Discipline (v21)

There was another alternative being offered to the church at Colossae – the way of discipline, more rules: do not handle, do not taste, do not touch, referring to things that all perish as they are used according to human precepts and teaching. But the problem with discipline is that it can lead to legalism in our lives. That's the context in which Paul speaks to them about Christ, 'In Christ all the fullness of the Godhead lives in bodily form' (Col. 2:9). I think the word 'fullness' was a key buzz word that these new teachers were using. They were saying 'What you need is the fullness that comes through philosophy' or 'religion' or 'mysticism' or 'discipline.' 'You need this extra fullness that will round you off in your Christian experience.' Paul is saying, 'Do you have Christ? Remember what happened at the very beginning of your Christian experience. You received him. As you received him, so continue in him, walk in him. When you get him you get, in him, all the fullness of the Godhead.'

In Christ, we have everything

That is the lead into what we're looking at: all the fullness dwells in Christ. In Christ, we have everything. That's the point he's making in chapter 1:15 and following. Paul begins by describing Jesus as the image of God. The Greek word is *icon*. Jesus is the exact likeness of God, like the image on the coin or the reflection in the mirror. The word also suggests that he is the manifestation of God: God is revealed perfectly in him. That is a very bold statement for Paul to make about Jesus within twenty-five years of Jesus' resurrection. He's telling us that these earliest Christians believed that Jesus is God.

I don't know if you've read Dan Brown and *The Da Vinci Code*. Dan Brown manipulates history for his own ends. He says in the book that people didn't believe in Jesus as God until about the third or fourth century. Up till then, they believed that Jesus was a man. But the real story is this: from the very earliest days, Christians believed that Jesus was God. The first big problem that the Christian church faced was not whether Jesus was divine, they accepted that, but whether Jesus, as divine, could also be fully human. Many people were influenced by Greek philosophy which said matter is evil. Everything to do with this realm, our bodies, the world we live in, the material universe, is evil. How could God ever take on human flesh and become a human being? That was the real issue.

Most of the gnostic gospels which Dan Brown quotes – and a new one was published recently, *The gospel according to Judas* – were about this very issue. The Jesus of *The gospel according to Judas*, for example, is a Jesus who doesn't believe that his flesh is part of him. He wants to get out of his flesh. He wants to die because the flesh is evil. And here's Paul making this categorical assertion, 'Yes, Jesus is God and God is in Christ.'

The Lordship of Christ

How extensive his Lordship is (vs 15-17)

Paul uses two phrases over and over again, 'he is' and 'all things.' 'He is the first born over all creation . . . by him all things are created. All things have been made by him. He is before all things. In him all things hold together. He has first place in everything. All the fullness is in him. And he's going to reconcile all things to himself.' What is left out? Nothing. Anything you can imagine is included in that; everything material, in heaven and on earth, in the spiritual realm where the authorities, the powers and the angels are. These mediatorial spirits that false teachers were talking about – all of that is under the control of Christ.

All things were made by him. He is above it all. He is the first born: that means he is before creation. It means that he is over creation. But more than anything else, this expression 'the first born' means that he is the heir of creation. It is his. God makes the universe and gives it to his Son. He is the heir of everything. That's what the phrase 'first born' means. The Jehovah's Witnesses are wrong to say 'First born means the first created' because (v16) 'by him all things were created.' Everything that existed comes from him as the originating centre, the spiritual locality, the conditioning clause. Everything comes in him or by him. Through him: he is the mediating agent through whom it happened and for him: he is the goal towards which everything exists. All of this is being said about Jesus, within a few years of his death and resurrection. Verse 17 sums up the thought of verses 15 and 16: 'He is before all things and in him, all things hold together.' He is the unifying principle and the personal sustainer of all creation.

Whenever I bump my head on a door frame or in getting into my car, I comfort myself in the fact that solid matter is not really solid. It's made up of space; a few little things whirling around that are called atoms that are held together by some indescribable, indefinable power. And the atom is made up of other things. It's made up of protons and neutrons and croûtons or something. But the thing that holds it all together is the Lord Jesus Christ. How extensive his Lordship is. There's nothing outside of his control.

How exclusive his Lordship is (vs 18,19)

This has particular relevance to the church at Colossae. Paul makes three claims for Jesus.

The head of the Body

To be the head means to be the sovereign, the chief, the leader. Paul is emphatic: Jesus is the Head of the church. He's the means of its existence. The church is under Christ. Paul was giving a charter of freedom to these Colossian Christians. These other people were imposing a guilt trip on them, saying, 'If you're going to be as spiritual as we are and experience what we've experienced, this is what you have to do. Don't handle, don't taste, don't touch . . .' Those were the mystics, the ascetics. Others were saying, 'If you want to be as spiritual as us, then you need to be as religious as we are. You need to keep holy days and recognise special sabbaths. You need to do what we tell you to do.' But Paul is saying, 'You don't have to be under any other master but Christ.' To know that Christ is the head is liberation for those of us who have been tyrannised by little people, who want to press us into their mould rather than lead us to Jesus.

The beginning and the first born from the dead

He has the precedence in the area of resurrection, this new eternal life. He's the Author of life. He's the beginning and the first born from the dead. Not only has he complete control in the world that we *can* see, but also in the world we *can't* see. In the realm of the eternal, he is Sovereign, so that in everything he might have supremacy.

The fullness of God

Paul says, 'For God was pleased to have all his fullness dwell in him.' 'What is it,' Paul is saying, 'about the words "all" and "fullness" that you don't understand? These people are saying, "Are you not satisfied in your Christian life?" And you're saying, "No." You don't feel as close to Jesus as you used to feel? What do you need? Something else? Something additional? Something extra? As you received Christ Jesus, so walk in him.'

You still need the same thing you needed at the beginning. You need Jesus and God is pleased to have all his fullness dwell in him. What have you got? You've got Jesus. 'You received him, remember?' he's saying. 'When you became a Christian, you received the Lord Jesus. Guess what you got with him? In him all the fullness of God dwells.' Don't let others bully you, making you feel guilty, trying to disqualify you because you don't measure up. If you have Christ, you have everything you need.

How effective his Lordship is (v20)

'Through him,' he says, (v20), 'to reconcile to himself all things, whether things on earth or things in heaven, by making peace through his blood shed on the cross.' He is moving us forward in his argument here. He's talked about the supremacy of the Lord Jesus and now he's stressing the sufficiency of the Lord Jesus. He has talked about creation (vs 15-17). By creation, he includes everything: the planets, the universe, all these things are included as the created order. And he's saying Christ is pre-eminent over creation.

Now the focus shifts (vs 18-21) and he's looking at the new creation: the church, the people of God. In verse 20, he talks about what Christ is doing for the body of the church. He has reconciled 'to himself all things, whether things on earth or things in heaven, by making peace through his blood, shed on the cross. Once you were alienated from God and were enemies in your minds because of your evil behaviour. But now he has reconciled you by Christ's physical body through death to present you holy in his sight' (v21).

This was revolutionary teaching in the first century world, that God, in Christ, should achieve this reconciliation by something he did in his physical body. What did he do? Chapter 2:13-14:'He forgave us all our sins, having cancelled the written code, with its regulations, that was against us and that stood opposed to us; he took it away, nailing it to the cross. And having disarmed the powers and authorities, he made a public spectacle of them, triumphing over them by the cross.'

Notice in Colossians 2, he is talking about the death of Jesus as a victory over the dark powers of this age. The theological description of that is *Christus victor*. Christ the victor, Christ the one in triumph over his enemies. What is it that gives these powers and authorities their influence over us? Our guilt, our sin; that's what gives the devil the right to go before God, as the accuser of the brothers and sisters, and accuse them before God. But what has happened to our sin? It has been taken. The debt we owe God because we have broken his law has been taken by the Lord Jesus and nailed to the cross. Jesus has taken what was against us on himself. He who was without sin was made sin for us, nailed to the cross. As I see my sin nailed to the cross, I see everything that was written against me nailed to that cross with him, in him, on him. The devil no longer has anything he can say.

Paul can write to the Romans and say, 'Who can bring a charge against God's elect? It is Christ who died.' There is only a victorious Jesus because there is a sin-bearing Jesus and there is only freedom for us from the powers of darkness because Jesus has paid the penalty for our sin, bearing sin in his own body on the tree. By doing that, he's reconciled us to God, by his blood on the cross. That's how effective his cross is and his Lordship is. This is Bible Christianity.

We have been estranged from God, we deserve to be judged and Jesus, by his death, has taken our place and we are given his right-eousness. That is a great challenge to things that are going on around us today, where people are, in the words of one person, 'Teaching a God without wrath, who brings men without sin, into a kingdom without righteousness, through the ministry of a Christ without a cross.' That's the new theology. Paul confutes that. Anyone who takes the Bible seriously finds that confuted by what the apostle is saying here to the Colossians.

If you read Colossians, you discover that the heart of the gospel is Christ. It's not sin. Some of us talk as if sin was the big issue, Christ is the big issue. We don't have to argue for sin, it's there in the Holocaust, the abortion clinic, the divorce court, the torture chamber, the abu-sive relationship, the office politics, the human heart and around the kitchen table. Sin is there. My heart is full of sin.

Christianity is Christ, that's what Colossians is proclaiming. It's all about Jesus. We can sum up the message to the Colossians: don't let anyone take you captive by introducing into Christianity some new philosophy. If you have Christ, you have all the fullness of God. Don't let anyone make you feel guilty: guilt is banished because the Lord Jesus took our place. This relationship that he has with us is a rela-tionship of grace. Don't let anyone disqualify you because the Lord Jesus Christ guarantees your right standing with God and your firm relationship with him. A dear Rwandan man, who had lost everything that he owned, said 'I didn't know that Jesus was all I needed, until Jesus was all I had.'

Ephesus
by Philip Hacking

Philip Hacking

Philip Hacking was minister of Christ Church, Fulwood, Sheffield, for many years and has also been involved with the Keswick Convention for over forty years, serving as the Chairman of the Convention Council. He has written several books, including the Keswick Study Guide, *Rhythm of the Gospel*. Now retired, he is a firm cricket fan.

Ephesus

Acts chapter 20

Introduction

I've been given Ephesus this week. Just about three weeks ago, I was doing a MasterSun Keswick Week in Samos. On one of the days, they had a trip to Ephesus, which isn't far away. It was all a ruin – the church of Ephesus went, long ago. The last reference in the Bible to the church in Ephesus is in the book of Revelation where the risen Lord says to the church in Ephesus: 'I have this against you, you've lost your first love.' The Christian church in Ephesus, as in the whole of that Asia Minor province, didn't die because the Islamic hordes came in and killed it. It died from within and then the Islamic hordes buried it.

I start with Acts 20 because Paul called in at Samos on his way to talk to the Ephesian elders in verse 17 onwards. He wants to remind them of his ministry. Paul spent more time in Ephesus than anywhere else. They had a tremendous history. You know how churches keep records of their previous ministers? I'm an Anglican, we do ours in odd ways, we hang our vicars in the vestry . . . well, we don't actually hang our vicars . . . I sometimes think we ought . . . but we don't, we hang the pictures of our vicars in the vestry. We remember the past and if you'd seen the role-call at Ephesus: Paul, Timothy, Apollos, John . . . my! What a list of preachers.

What was Paul talking about to these Ephesian elders? Verse 20: '. . . I've taught you publicly and from house to house. I've not hesitated to preach anything that would be helpful.' His prime ministry was to teach, publicly and from house to house. He preaches that they must turn to God in repentance and have faith in our Lord Jesus. He could say therefore he (v26) was innocent of the blood of all men. The task of every Christian who has any pastoral responsibilities is to make sure that as far as we know, we've taught the Word of God and we're innocent of the blood of all men. It was hard work. Paul talks about the hard work that he had to do (vs 33–35) – he worked part time with his hands so that he might be free from having to be supported. And more than that, verses 19 and 31, his ministry was 'with tears.' It was costly. His three years' ministry cost a great deal and now he knew that he was moving on.

Chapters 18 and 19: here is the ministry. Ephesus was an important city and it was strategic. If you won Ephesus, then your message would spread. Paul's original plan in Acts 16 was to go straight to Ephesus, sow the seed in the centre and then let it spread. But God had other plans, and so Paul went through Philippi, and did it the other way round. Last of all he went to this centre, which became the centre of the church in Asia. This preaching went on for two years (Acts 19:10), 'so that all the Jews and Greeks who lived in the province of Asia heard the word of the Lord.' There was such a spread that you could say they'd all heard.

I am an Anglican and I've served actively in three different churches. It was always my tradition that it was my responsibility to all those thousands of people who lived in my parish that they were made aware of the reality of the truth of the word of God. I failed miserably. But at least I tried. Whatever denomination you are, we have a responsibility to make sure that the word spreads. When the church is only looking after itself, it's finished and sometimes we're quite content just to keep the show on the road. We've no great vision. I sometimes see strategies and all too often they are how to cut down the number of ministers, how to save money so that we can survive, whereas the ministry of Paul in Ephesus was to see that the word spread out and out.

A plan to be pursued

Does your church plan? I hope you're not content just to tick over. There was a long term plan but there was also a short term plan. What did happen in Ephesus was very intriguing. Chapter 18:19, they arrived in Ephesus, where Paul left Priscilla and Aquila, two godly people who'd been with him in Corinth. He leaves them at Ephesus to be a church plant. They began their home and their witness amongst their fellow Jews and this was part of the plan. Later on, in verses 24-26

> . . . a Jew named Apollos, a native of Alexandria, came to Ephesus. He was a learned man, with a thorough knowledge of the Scriptures. He had been instructed in the way of the Lord, and he spoke with great fervour and taught about Jesus accurately, though he knew only the baptism of John. He began to speak boldly in the synagogue. When Priscilla and Aquila heard him, they invited him to their home and explained to him the way of God more adequately.

Apollos was humble enough to learn and he became a great and godly leader.

This church plant was two ordinary people who'd worked alongside Paul in Corinth. He'd placed them in a new situation and they find a man with great gifts who could do what they couldn't do and they helped him to get the message. We must plant churches and put out our best people. I was talking to a vicar who was thinking of sending fifty people away to start a new church. And he said, 'I can think of the fifty I would send away gladly to start a new church!' We want the people who are the best people to start the new church. Priscilla and Aquila planted and the short term plan meant that when Paul eventually got to Ephesus, he's got a group ready.

A power to be proved

Power in conversion

Chapter 19:1-7; there were some disciples who only knew John's baptism but hadn't received the Spirit. Paul placed hands on them (v6) and they spoke in tongues and prophesied and entered into a genuine experience. What do we do about the dead churches littered all over our country? There are so many of them. Do we just forget them? I think we need to longingly pray that life may come into deadness. How wonderful it would be if we saw that kind of conversion experience.

Power in proclamation

Paul began and spoke in the synagogue 'for three months, arguing persuasively about the kingdom of God' (Acts 19:8). Here he was in Ephesus, a big city with a large Jewish contingent and he starts with them, trying to convince them that the Messiah had come. 'Some of them became obstinate; they refused to believe' (v9). Some people find it hard to believe and they're genuine. But there are very many people who refuse to believe, who hide behind this word 'agnostic.' It's not that they can't believe, they don't *want* to believe. How could anybody possibly believe the *Da Vinci Code* and not the gospel? Only the person who's absolutely perverse. There isn't evidence for it, not the slightest, but the *Da Vinci Code* doesn't change my life one little bit. I can believe it all and enjoy it but it doesn't change my life. If I believe the gospel my life will be changed.

Paul '. . . took the disciples with him and had discussions daily in the lecture hall of Tyrannus.' While we pray for life to come to dead churches, we do not have time to wait for dead churches to come alive. We've got to take the initiative. Travelling around in ministry now, I see it so abundantly. Paul lectured and was doing a job and yet day by day by day for two years, he taught and taught. And while Ephesus didn't keep their revival, I believe one of the greatest needs of our day is for a teaching ministry so the people get to know the word of God in depth, so that we can face the ideas, the new religions that are always springing up.

Power in liberation

Chapter 19:11 onwards; 'God did extraordinary miracles through Paul.' Ephesus was a place where there was a lot of magic: this great temple to Diana, one of the seven wonders of the ancient world. And because of that, God worked in unusual ways. I don't think it's normal that handkerchiefs should be left out in a superstitious way, hoping that miracles would be wrought. But in that particular situation, God used that unusual means. In verse 13 onwards you get the story of exorcisms, demons being cast out.

> When this became known to the Jews and Greeks living in Ephesus, they were all seized with fear, and the name of the Lord Jesus was held in high honour. Many of those who believed now came and openly confessed their evil deeds. A number who had practised sorcery brought their scrolls together and burned them publicly. When they calculated the value of the scrolls, the total came to fifty thousand drachmas. In this way the word of the Lord spread widely and grew in power (Acts 19:17-21).

When I became a Christian, we didn't live much on this level. Today, we do. There are Satanist and pagan chaplains in universities, Satanists want their place on *Thought for the Day* on BBC; after all it's a faith. If we are going to see God at work there will need to be liberation in these cases. The majority of our people of our land don't need that but there are many who are brought into the work of the evil one, who need to be freed. These things are becoming abundantly true. I have a son who acts as a vicar and he tells me some of the things that they encounter in his Church of England school from some of the kids. They know far more about the activity of Satan than they do about the activity of God.

A price to be paid

It was costly. There was a great riot. Why? Verse 23, 'there arose a great disturbance about the Way.' A silversmith who was making images of

Diana found that his job was less lucrative. People weren't buying images any more because they were being converted. It hit the commercial interest.

I did ten years of my ministry in Scotland and had the joy of travelling around with a great man, Duncan Campbell, who had been around in the great revival in the Hebrides. His big line was this: 'When did opposition begin in the Hebrides after the revival? When the whisky sales began to drop.' When people got a different spirit to inspire them, the spirit trade began to fall. Once the commercial interests begin to be disturbed, opposition comes. So the church in Ephesus began to be attacked.

There was a price to be paid by the pastor as well. We have four illustrations of what Paul went through at Ephesus.

The plots of the Jews

In chapter 20:19, Paul says, 'I was severely tested by the plots of the Jews.' We don't know what they were: they're not mentioned in the narrative. Perhaps these people who couldn't fight against the truth decided they'd shut the mouth of the man who preached it. Friends, if you think you live in a world where that doesn't happen any more, you don't know what's happening in church politics.

Fighting wild beasts

1 Corinthians 15:32 says: 'If I fought wild beasts in Ephesus for merely human reasons, what have I gained?' Fought wild beasts in Ephesus? There is no reference to this in Acts. Was he thrown into the arena? Possibly. Or was he using it metaphorically – the opposition was so strong it was like going against wild beasts? I think it's the latter, they acted against him so angrily. Have you ever wondered why the world hates Christians? Jesus said, 'If they hate me, they will hate you as well.' Why did they hate Jesus? The truth, when it's proclaimed courageously and sacrificially, will win some but it will produce hatred.

I speak now to a lot of younger ministers and I always say, 'Make your mind up. If you decide, when you go to your church, you will always preach a message that is popular and doesn't drive anybody away from your church, then forget the gospel. If you're prepared to have people leave the church, you'll have people born again.' I always found it very hurtful when people moved away from my church, not because we'd done something wrong but because they didn't honestly like the message. I remember a lady who'd come for a few weeks and then stopped coming. I went to see her. I said, 'Can you tell me why you don't come?' 'I've travelled around with my husband all over the country and I always go to the local Church of England and you're the first one that's told me I must be born again. How do I know you're right and they're wrong?' I said, 'It's not about whether I'm right and they're wrong, what does the Bible say?' But she didn't want to know. She wanted a church which told her what she wanted to hear. And there always will be that kind of opposition.

An open door

Glance over to 1 Corinthians 16:8. Paul writing from Ephesus '. . . I will stay on at Ephesus until Pentecost, because a great door for effective work has opened to me, and there are many who oppose me.' Do you see that balance? 'I'm staying here,' said Paul, after three years, 'as long as it's right, because there's a great door but there's a great door for the opponents.'

I had a friend who ministered in the early days in Albania when the door opened in that atheistic country. And he said how wonderful it was: the gospel got in. But it didn't take long for all the false cults or the pornography to get in as well. The same door that let in the gospel let in the opponents of the gospel. And you will always expect an open door, yes, but an open door for both good and evil.

Despairing of life

2 Corinthians 1:8-9: 'We do not want you to be uninformed, brothers, about the hardships we suffered in the province of Asia. We were under great pressure, far beyond our ability to endure, so that we despaired even of life. Indeed, in our hearts we felt the sentence of death.' What does that mean? I think it means he was deeply depressed, even suicidal in thought. Life itself had no meaning any more. I don't think he means that he was under sentence of death

by the powers that be, and for any who've gone through deep depression, I hope it comes of some comfort that this man understood it.

Ephesians the letter

Sit

One of the most telling commentaries on Ephesians is called *Sit, Walk, Stand*, by Watchman Nee, a man who did suffer for his faith. The first three chapters of Ephesians are Sit: the riches of Christ, the truth which included not just peace with God but peace between man and man. That's why Jews and Greeks are mentioned constantly in Acts as coming together in Ephesus across the boundaries; across the racial distinctions. I still remember one of the most moving Bible studies I ever took was in Londonderry, Northern Ireland. I took a Bible study with four prisoners from the Maze prison; two Protestants, two Roman Catholic; two Unionists, two Republicans. One of the Republicans said, 'Isn't it strange. If I'd not become a Christian in that prison I'd have been after his life as soon as we got out and now we're brothers in Christ.' What a wonderful testimony that it can break down murderous barriers.

Walk

In chapters 4 and 5, you get the Walk bit. It's the tremendous challenge to Christians to walk worthy (4:1) and to walk in love (5:2). That's the way Christians are meant to be, to walk as children of light (v8). The Christian life is the continuing steady work. If you don't keep walking with him then things will go wrong.

I was privileged to preach at my senior grandson's wedding last Saturday. They wanted me to preach on Ephesians 5, that passage about husbands and wives. I pointed out to them that this bit is all part of walking worthy, walking in love. It's the steady, daily, regular, relationship with God. In Ephesus, what mattered was not who founded it, not the exciting things that happened at the beginning, but the walk. And things sometimes went wrong.

Stand

The stand bit is chapter 6:10 onwards – spiritual warfare. We hear a lot about that these days. 'Be strong in the Lord, in the power of his might.' Somebody said that it's interesting the spiritual warfare bit in Ephesians comes immediately after the instructions about the family. Very often the biggest battles are in the family. Satan's been trying to destroy family life for a long time and he's doing very well indeed. Sooner or later, the person living in a normal, nuclear family will be the exception rather than the rule.

Spiritual warfare very often does mean the family but it's much more than that. If I enjoy the riches of Christ, if I walk in love, then there's a fight on. I'm still young enough to want to be involved in the fight. If I'm a servant of Christ, I shall be that till I can do it no more. Whatever age we are, there is a battle on, and I hope you're ready for the fight because there will be a fight. To escape the fight is to escape following Jesus.

How does the letter end? It ends on a most lovely benediction (v24) 'Grace to all who love our Lord Jesus Christ with an undying love.' Then, the last time the Ephesian church is mentioned, 'I have this against you, that you have lost your first love.' The church in Ephesus was still sound; it believed and cared about the right things, but it had lost its love. How do you keep true, pure, orthodox and yet loving? Only when you know the infilling of the Spirit.

I had a friend who loved reading Keswick sermons and he said Ephesians 5:18 was the most preached-on text in the Keswick Convention: 'Keep on being filled in the Spirit.' The only way in which the church could go on sitting, walking, standing is if they kept on being filled with the Spirit. The only way in which Keswick will go on doing God's will is when it keeps on being filled with the Spirit. Thank God it's happening. May it continue. The only way in which the church in Britain or overseas will continue to prosper is when we keep on being filled with the Spirit of Jesus who brings us riches, who helps us to sit, walk and stand.

Famous last words – John

A serving community

by Steve Brady

Steve Brady

Steve Brady was born and educated in Liverpool, where he was converted in his teens. He trained at what is now the London School of Theology, where he met Brenda, his wife of thirty years! They have two children, Paul and Ruth, and two grandchildren, Daniel and Annabelle.

A serving community

John 13

Introduction

Most early Saturday evenings in our home were spent with our young family, before they went to bed, eating pizza and watching *The A Team*. If you had a problem and no one else could help, and you could find them, you could hire 'The A Team.' It had incredible plots, all basically the same: the bad guys were beating somebody up, the good guys came along and then got thrown into some little shed somewhere with enough equipment to build a tank, and then it all turned out right in the end.

Here in the gospel of John, the first twelve chapters have dealt with three years of Jesus' life and the following nine chapters then deal with his next few days. Within twenty-four hours, Jesus will be dead. Yet according to John's Gospel, he is like God's 'A Team', the one who comes to rescue people who are held in the bondage of sin, whose lives are falling apart, under the dominion of evil and power of the devil. The Lord Jesus comes to deal with destruction, despair and death itself, so that men and women may be liberated to enjoy God forever.

As we come to this passage, we have this astonishing story of a very menial task. In the Ancient Middle East, if you went out for a meal or party, you'd have a bath before you went. When you got to your destination, all you would need was perhaps your hands to be washed and definitely your feet, as the roads were dusty. But to wash feet was a menial task. Luke's Gospel reminds us that there was heated discussion going on amongst the disciples. It was about who was the greatest. Who in the kingdom of Jesus was going to be the most important? Who was going to be a cabinet minister? Who were going to be princes and rulers over parts of the kingdom? It was all about I, me, myself and personally. Can you imagine it? The Son of God is going to the cross and they are trying to work out who should be getting the best seats in what they understood at the time to be the imminent coming of his kingdom that would promote them to high office.

But Jesus does the unimaginable. He divests himself of his outer garments, he wraps himself with a towel, and then he stoops and humbly washes their feet. In the midst of it, Peter says, 'Lord, are you going to wash my feet?' Jesus replies, 'You do not realise now what I am doing, but later you will understand' (v7). Let's approach this passage through the lens of this verse.

Be glad for what you can know

Here is the major thing I want us to see from this text: be glad for what you can know. In the gospels, we have not only the words but the works of Jesus, his gracious words and his mighty deeds, and this is one of his deeds. In the Gospel of John alone there are some mighty and miraculous deeds: changing water into wine, feeding the five thousand, raising Lazarus from the dead etc. But there are other deeds of Jesus – riding into Jerusalem on a donkey or clearing out the temple. They are not miraculous deeds, but they are still the deeds of Jesus and they too have a purpose. The foot washing ministry of Jesus is an acted parable; it is significant, it is a pointer to something.

We read that it was just before the Passover feast (13:1). Jesus 'knew that his time [literally his 'hour'] had come.' He is now just hours away from his 'midnight', his approaching death. His whole career, right through the Gospel of John, has been about the 'hour', and now it has come.

'Jesus knew that the Father had put all things under his power, and that he had come from God and was returning to God' (v3). He got up from the meal, just like he had risen from his eternal throne. Then he did a remarkable thing – he took off his outer garments; or as John 17 puts it, he had laid aside his glory (v5). And then he put a towel around himself, a mark of his servanthood, a humble servant. It's John 1:14 being parabled before us: the Word who was God (v1) became flesh and dwelt amongst us as a servant (see Phil. 2:6-8).

Bono's recently produced a book, *Bono on Bono*, which is a series of conversations with a journalist. In it, he relates how he had just returned from a trip to Tokyo. He is very tired and jet-lagged but he goes along to St Patrick's Cathedral in Dublin, to a carol service where he's falling asleep. Suddenly realisation kicks in

> It dawned on me for the first time, really. It had dawned on me before, but it really sank in: the Christmas story. The idea that God, if there is a force of Love and Logic in the universe, that it would seek to explain itself is amazing enough. That it would seek to explain itself and describe itself by becoming a child born in straw poverty . . . a child . . . I just thought: "Wow!" Just the poetry . . . Unknowable love, unknowable power, describes itself as the most vulnerable. There it was. I was sitting there, and it's not that it hadn't struck me before, but tears came down my face, and I saw the genius of this, utter genius of picking a particular point in time, and deciding to turn on this . . . It's actually logical. It's pure logic. Essence has to manifest itself. It's inevitable. Love has to become an action or something concrete. It would have had to happen. There must be an incarnation. Love must be made flesh.[1]

In the couplets of two carols:

> Lo, within the manger lies,
> He who built the starry skies.

> Our God contracted to a span,
> Incomprehensibly made man!

That's not the whole story. With a towel around himself, Jesus stooped down and washed the disciples' feet. Why? Peter's having none of it, and off he goes to the other extreme: 'Lord, not only my feet, but my hands and everything else.' Jesus says: 'A person who has had a bath needs only to wash his feet; his whole body is clean' (v10).

What's he talking about? The gospel, the story of himself. He's going to a cross and there he is going to suffer and die for his creatures' sin, and having died for them, he will be raised majestically. Through his death he provides a bath, a washing, a cleansing, for men and women who are dirty, defiled, sinful and rebellious. The sheer genius that the eternal God steps into this seemingly insignificant planet to put it right. Jesus literally washed dirty feet, and truly cleanses dirty souls. Then he returns to his place; just as through his death and ascension he has returned to our Father's right hand as our great God and Saviour, Jesus Christ. This is the gospel, the good news. We can be clean through one who stooped to a cross to make us so.

Jesus asks, 'Do you understand what I have done for you' (v12)? Do you understand what the Lord Jesus has done for you? Do you understand this big story of the gospel? This is the heart of it: that the Almighty God has become one of us, stepping into our skin and size and space and shape; he dies for our sin so that we might be forgiven and welcomed into his forever family and his everlasting kingdom.

Be humble for what you don't know

Jesus says to Peter, 'You do not realise now what I am doing, but later you will understand' (v7). There are some versions of Christian faith that suggest that if you become a Christian, all your problems will be solved, all your questions will be answered and you will have a perpetual 32 teeth grin because you know that no matter what is happening in life, you have the inside track. You're not in the crowd on the platform at the railway station. Instead, God says, 'Come and sit here in the signal box. Look, "This is why that is delayed, and this is why the other is delayed, and now you understand the secrets of the universe."'

I don't know what Bible you read to get that idea. This Bible says that there are certain things on this side of heaven that we do not know. 'What I am doing *now*', says Jesus to Peter 'you do not know.' Christians are not people who have the inside track on everything that is going on in the world. When I became a Christian, the next day friends were asking questions that I would have needed to be a walking Christian Encyclopaedia Britannica to answer. I didn't know then, and I have lots and lots of things that I still don't know. We live in the *now*.

Some of us have are facing big questions. 'Why did God let my Granny die?' 'Why did I have to be the one to get that diagnosis of cancer?' 'Why did I have to fail that exam and get a third rate choice to go to a fourth rate university?' 'I always thought he would keep his wedding vows. I'm here tonight with a broken heart and a broken marriage and the kids are distraught and I don't know what to do as daddy isn't coming home.' 'Where is God in all the turmoil of what I call my life?'

We're a bit like Job: unaware that behind the scenes, God is working it altogether for the good of those who love him. We feel like we are in some 'A Team' plot and that it has all gone wrong. Will there be a happy ending; will we be rescued? Where is God when life is so hard? Faith is not freedom from problems, temptation or even doubt; faith is calling upon God and trusting Jesus no matter what.

Be patient for what you will know

Notice the pattern of 'now, later, now, later' in this passage? 'Peter, what I'm doing in washing your feet and all that it signifies, you don't understand now, but later you will.' In its immediate context, it is pointing to the cross and the resurrection. Jesus is saying 'Peter, what is going on in this acted parable you'll be able to figure out when I have died and risen again to life.' But in the light of the cross, Christians also live in a 'now and a not yet', a 'now' and a 'hereafter' as the Authorised Version has it. It is the tension of the Bible – the kingdom has come in Jesus but not yet in all its fullness.

I can remember twenty-seven years ago next month, on holiday in Scotland, pushing a pram with our eight-month-old son in it, and stopping and saying to my wife, 'Brenda, I have something to tell you. Just sit down for a minute.' I'd taken three months to pick the time and the opportunity to say to my young wife that she had an incurable disease called Multiple Sclerosis. We thought that we were facing wheelchairs and death. Twenty-seven years on, by the grace of God, she is still pressing on. At that time, the Lord laid this verse on my wife's heart and mine independently: 'What I am doing now you do not know. You shall hereafter.' There have been times when I've hoped that God would turn up and say 'Now you see why, don't you?'

Sometimes, in God's mercy, when you are going through something, just a wee bit further along the road of life you look back and see why. For instance, many of you know that I am from Liverpool. From the age of eleven, I had to learn Latin, and French, which was amazing because I had to learn English as a foreign language! And then aged twelve, I had the choice of Geography, German or Greek. This was a no-brainer. I wanted to do German because my Dad had spent five years in a German 'holiday camp', Stalag 8B, having been wounded and captured at Dunkirk in 1940. He spoke German fluently. However, I was not to tell my school that. 'Now listen, lad, don't you tell 'em that I know German, 'cos they'll expect too much from you.' 'OK, Dad.' Teacher: 'Why do you want to do German?' 'I like languages.' 'Oh, you like languages, do you? Well get this, you're going to do Greek.' I thought the sky had fallen in. I hated that wretched language. But four years later, I became a Christian. I discovered that the New Testament was written in Greek, and a few years later, because I had an 'O' level in Greek, I was allowed to do a degree in theology without any of the then necessary 'A' levels. I understood that 'frowning providence' a bit further down the road of life. I still thank God for it.

But what happens when heaven is silent? A loved one, instead of rising like Lazarus from the grave, is taken from you. In spite of all the prayer, nothing changes. 'What I am doing now you do not know, but later you will understand.' Do you believe that? Wasn't it lovely that Nigel Lee, who was due to be with us at Keswick this year, wrote the following during his final illness: 'Our trials have included much glory through the kindness of the Lord.' His last words to the Keswick Convention were, 'And the best is yet to come.' Because of Jesus it is so.

Get on then with what you do know

Verses 13-15: Jesus says 'I have set you an example that you should do as I have done.' The word example here is an interesting word. Years ago my wife bought one of those DIY carpet kits. You only have to stitch in, I don't know, fifty thousand strands? Then you get a beautiful carpet. She started well, then we used to send it birthday cards as the years rolled by. I think it was getting ready to collect its pension! The process towards completion seemed so slow. But it had a pattern, all the different colours, and where they were supposed to go. As she stitched them in, a picture began to emerge. One day a kind friend stepped in and finished the carpet for us. Beautiful! Jesus says, 'I've left you a pattern like that, something to stitch into, so that a picture of me may be formed through you.'

There are some Christians who practise foot-washing literally. I've experienced it a few times and it's very humbling. But what is Jesus saying? Go and wash feet? No. Jesus says, 'I have given you a pattern, a picture.' What is the principle? If you study the Bible academically, you learn big phrases like 'ladders of abstraction.' What's a ladder of abstraction? It's when you take a passage and you abstract from it its principles. Is that legitimate? Yes. Foot washing was a cultural way of serving someone in need in the Middle East where the roads were dusty. Jesus says, 'I have given you a pattern so that you learn what it is to take on the menial, the humdrum, just as I, your Lord and Master, took on a servant's role.' Jesus is saying 'You know enough; now get on with what you do know.'

In the film *First Knight*, Arthur and Lancelot enter the council chamber of the round table whose motto is: 'Here we believe that every life is precious, even the lives of strangers. If you must die, die serving something greater than yourself.' The world asks: how many people serve you? That's the position of status: 'I have three thousand people who work for/serve me in my company.' For Jesus, the key question is: how many people do you serve? Jesus is saying that if I, the Lord of heaven and earth, have stooped to serve you, then you also need to serve others. You may have to nurse someone near and dear who is in the early stages of Alzheimer's disease or latter stages of cancer. For you, it may be young children, aged parents, a friend, work colleague or neighbour in need, whom you are called to serve in seemingly menial tasks. You are not in the limelight; only God really knows and understands what you have to do. Will you do it for Jesus? Will you?

As we close, I wonder whether you are 'sinking' or 'thinking' under all the weight of the unexplained in your life? 'Sinking' as you look at the menial or 'thinking' about Jesus, the perfect servant, who is able to give you the grace to 'wash feet' for him. Sinking or thinking: your choice will make all the difference to another's world, your own and the world hereafter.

Endnote

1 *Bono on Bono: Conversations with Michka Assayas* (London: Hodder & Stoughton, 2005), p125.

A fruitful community – John 15

by Derek Tidball

Derek Tidball

Derek has been Principal of the London School of Theology (formerly London Bible College) since 1995 and was elected Chairman of the Council of the Evangelical Alliance in 2004. He has served as a pastor of two Baptist churches and began teaching at LBC in 1972. He was President of the Baptist Union 1990-1991 and became a Vice-President of the Evangelical Alliance in 1995. For four years, he was the Head of the Mission Department of the Baptist Union.

Derek is the author of twenty books and edits the Bible Themes series of the BST books for IVP. He is a regular preacher at many international Bible Conventions.

A Fruitful Community – John 15

Introduction

I am a bit of a Philistine when it comes to gardening. When Di and I bought the last house that we lived in, we deliberately chose a house that had a pocket handkerchief sized garden at the back because we never have time to do any gardening. If we do have leisure time, there are other things we prefer to be doing, so my experience of gardening is that it is mostly fighting back the wilderness! It gets so chaotic that I never see anything positive grow, except by accident, because I have to restrain the overgrowth and the weeds. But God has a sense of humour and the principal's house at the London School of Theology, in which we currently live, has not one or two gardens but four. We are surrounded by gardens, and as far as I'm concerned there is nothing that a good dose of concrete wouldn't cure!

The picture Jesus uses

Agricultural metaphors don't come naturally to me. However, they were very natural to Jesus. When Jesus uses the image of his Father as the gardener or the vinedresser and him being the vine, it wasn't just because he was wandering down the street in Jerusalem and saw some of the spectacular vines for which it is famous. He was picking up a 'metaphor of history'; when Jesus uses these words he was digging deep back into the psyche of Israel.

A symbol of Israel

Let me introduce you to the picture that Jesus uses, as his original hearers would have been familiar with it. When he says in John 15:1 that 'my Father is the gardener' they'd have thought that there was nothing objectionable about that – because grapes and Israel go together like fish and chips. When the spies in Numbers 13 went to explore the Promised Land, they came back and said that there were giants in the land; everything seemed to be very large. And what did they bring back with them? A single cluster of grapes so big that two of them carried it on a pole between them. Here is a metaphor that stood as a symbol for Israel, and down through their history the prophets preached about it. They picked up this image and used it time and time again.

If you wandered through the temple in Jesus' day, you would have noticed over its porch was a golden vine trailing as a sign of God's provision and abundant grace to them. If you'd wandered down towards the Kidron Valley, you would have seen clusters of grapes. When they revolted against Rome and minted their own coinage, they put a vine onto the coins as a symbol of their identity.

There are frequent Old Testament allusions to Israel as a vine. Sometimes it's used in a positive way to speak of the privileges of Israel and the grace of God towards Israel. In Psalm 80:8-9 and in Isaiah 5:1, God says Israel was a choice people; he planted them on a fertile hillside, using the choicest vines, the best plants that he could find. Ezekiel 17:5-8 picks up the same theme. Ezekiel said to Israel 'You were planted by God in good soil by abundant water so that Israel would bear fruit and become a splendid vine' (paraphrased).

Sadly, that same image that speaks of the abundant love of God for his chosen people was also used to speak of the failures of Israel. Isaiah 5:2 immediately introduces the problem: planted well by those abundant waters, the roots went down, but then the roots started growing in the wrong direction. Israel started following after idols and other gods and 'yielded only bad fruit'. Hosea uses the same picture to say that they had become self-indulgent.

A sign in Cana

This metaphor then digs deep into the history of the Old Testament and when Jesus says 'my Father is the gardener' his listeners would have linked what he was saying back to the Old Testament prophets. But he then goes on to say that he was the vine, (v5): 'I am the vine: you are the branches.' He grafts his actions into the sign of the vine as the symbol of Israel; as is seen, for example, in the sign that he gave at Cana in John 2.

John's Gospel is incredibly structured. There are seven miracles, called signs in John's Gospel and there are seven 'I am' sayings that go with them. Often the action and the saying are simultaneous – for example, the 'I am the resurrection and the life' saying occurs in the episode of the raising of Lazarus. But occasionally, like here, you get the action in one place and the saying and explanation come later. In John 2, Jesus goes to a family wedding in Cana and they run out of wine. Mary pushes Jesus forward and says her son will sort the situation out. 'No, it's not my time yet.' He responds only to the call of God.

Even so, Jesus invites the servants to take the great jars that they would have used for the cleansing ritual before the guests ate at the feast, and he tells them to fill them with water and then he turns the water into the wine – 185 gallons of it – such is the generosity of God. But where was the water to be found that was transformed into wine? It was to be found in the old great jars that were used to obey the old law of Israel, the ritual laws of cleansing. In that act Jesus is saying that the old water, the old laws of Israel, had now passed. A new day of the wine of the kingdom has come. He says Israel, having failed in its mission, is now going to have that mission fulfilled by Jesus himself and by the community of disciples that he had drawn around him; this is the time of the good grape.

What Jesus did in John 2 is picked up and explained all these chapters later in John 15. That isn't all that can be said about the role and future of Israel. Paul mentions something more of their story and future in Romans 9-11, but that's the image that is being used here.

The purpose Jesus announces

'My father is the gardener' . . . 'I am the vine' . . . and . . . 'you (are to go and) bear much fruit.' He says that twice in verse 5 and again in verse 8, and comes back to it in verse 16. 'You are to go and bear fruit, fruit that will last.' That is the purpose of being a branch, being connected with the vine.

There was nothing particularly smart about the soccer I used to play at school. The little town where I grew up had all the hallmarks of German bombing in my childhood. We tended to play on what was still a bombsite. We had no kit and no boots to speak of. We used to line up in the playground and the master would choose two team captains and they would pick the people they wanted. That usually meant, if they were wise, that Tidball came at the end! Every now and again people made a mistake and they chose me early. But that's when the problems started. If they chose you early they chose you for a particular job, they wanted you to play in a certain position, to either score goals or defend the goal. You were chosen to accomplish a mission. And they were sorry when they chose me!

So it is with the calling of the church. When did the churches last score or, to change the image, bear fruit for Jesus? Many churches exist year after year without seeing any converts. That was the problem. Israel wasn't being fruitful, and if she did produce fruit it was rotten fruit and she gorged herself on it. Israel did not sow the world with God's righteousness as he had intended them to do.

Isaiah 27:6 says that in the days to come 'Jacob will take root, Israel will bud and blossom and fill all the world with fruit.' You and I are the new Israel who are called to be the fruit bearers for God. We are called to bear much lasting fruit. We are now his friends, in on the inner circle. That's what Jesus says in verse 16; we are his friends and chosen, appointed, so that we may go and bear fruit.

It's a badge of great honour. Think of those shops or companies in London where they can put the royal crest outside and say that by royal appointment the sovereign has chosen them to supply the royal family with snuff or whatever: they're proud of this royal appointment. Everyone here in the tent tonight is here by divine appointment, chosen to go and bear fruit. Donald Rumsfeld won the 'Campaign for Plain English Award' in 2003. In a press conference in the United States he said, 'As you know, there are some knowns and some unknown knowns. We also know that there are known unknowns but there are also some unknown unknowns, ones we don't know we don't know.' Now here is a known known from Jesus. What Jesus says is perfectly clear, it's plain enough: 'You have been appointed to go and bear fruit.'

Fruit-bearing as evangelism

What is this fruit-bearing? Part of it is speaking the gospel and sharing the message of salvation. Paul picks up that image in Colossians 1:6 'All over the world the gospel is bearing fruit and growing.' Praise God, that is still true today. There are places, like Europe, where the gospel is making progress slowly but through the church of God the gospel is spreading rapidly in most parts of the world. We Europeans are the ones who are left behind at the moment.

Fruit-bearing as social justice

Part of this is the task of fruit-bearing and evangelism in getting the message of Jesus across. Part of fruit-bearing is the fruit of justice. In the original context, in Isaiah 5 where Israel was introduced as the vine, Isaiah went on to say, in verses 8-26, that God looked for justice and for righteousness but all he heard were the cries of the weak, cries of distress and oppression.

We ought to be a people who engage vigorously in the evangelistic task of proclaiming the crucified Christ, but we ought also to be a people engaged in the righteousness of the kingdom and who reveal the just heart of our Father Creator.

Fruit-bearing as personal holiness

Another part of this fruit-bearing is the fruit of personal holiness. Your mind has probably already gone to Galatians 5:22 where the fruit of the Spirit is spoken of, with those nine different qualities. I always think it's like one of those blended fruit juices that boasts on the carton you'll taste banana and coconut and a whole range of other fruits. You and I are called to demonstrate the blended fruit of holiness in our lives: not to be selective and say we'll specialise in some of them whereas others will specialise in others. We need to have all of them blended together in our personal character; the love and joy and peace, the patience and kindness and goodness, the faithfulness and the gentleness and the self control. You can't say 'I'm all right because I'm a joyful personality. I'm always praising God, I'm an extrovert, and so I'll say hallelujah even on the darkest days,' when actually those around you need someone to weep with them. You are also called to gentleness.

I'm an extremely self-disciplined person, I'm told. Self-control comes easily to me; in fact, some of my students wonder whether I am a person or a machine! Self-control might come naturally to me, but I have to also remember that I'm called to patience, one of the other aspect of the fruit of the Spirit, with those who find it difficult to get going.

In all these ways we are called to be fruit-bearers and to produce fruit *that will last*.

What will be the legacy of your life? What will you be remembered for? In the film *About Schmidt*, the lead character, Warren Schmidt, played by Jack Nicholson, is coming to the end of his life. He's just retired and he's looking back, and in the final sequence in the film he is reflecting on what he has achieved in his life. 'What difference have I made in someone's life?' he asks himself, and then he says, sadly, 'None that I can think of, none at all.' What legacy will you leave behind? What fruit you will leave?

The principles Jesus teaches

What are the secrets of such fruit-bearing? John 15 gives us the principles of spiritual horticulture. There are four to bear in mind.

Pruning

Verse 2 tells us. 'He cuts off every branch that bears no fruit. Every branch that does bear fruit he prunes so that it will be even more fruitful.' The Jews went in for a double pruning. In April and May the dead branches were cut out of the vines and then in July and August the weak branches were taken out to allow the strong branches to produce greater, stronger clusters of grapes.

If we want to be fruitful, there is no getting away from the fact that it will require a pruning by God. This comes in various ways. Maybe it comes from opposition and conflict. Jesus goes on from John chapter 18 onwards to say that this is going to be the fate of his disciples. Maybe the pruning comes as you read the word of God and you are convicted about certain aspects of your life. Maybe it comes from the people of God moulding and shaping you and challenging you in love about certain aspects of your life. Or maybe it comes through the ordinary circumstances of life, as you look back at the failures and disappointments and they drive you to God. Fruitfulness usually comes where pruning has taken place. Alistair Begg, speaking about Joseph, reminded us that when we shun trials we are going to miss blessings. He uses this phrase that I've often repeated: 'When all you have is sunshine, then all you get is desert.'[1] We need the hard times, for spiritual fruit arises from them.

Remaining (v4)

The simple secret of fruitfulness is to stay close to Jesus, to stay connected, to remain in him. Then he promises 'I will remain in you' (v4). Only as we are connected to Jesus can we be fruitful.

Asking (v7)

Verse 7: asking grows naturally out of intimacy. When you have a good relationship as a son with your father you don't hold back, you ask boldly for things. You have the confidence to ask that arises out of intimacy. Verse 7 seems to give us Christians a blank cheque: 'If you remain in me and my words remain in you, ask whatever you wish, and it will be given you.' This is not a blank cheque because, if you remain in Jesus, you know that there are certain things not to ask for! If you are remaining in Jesus then your wishes will be formed by your relationship with him. But I can't help thinking that many of us, as James says, 'do not have because we do not ask.'[2] We don't have the boldness of faith to make us fruit-bearing Christians; we are content the way we are. Every great revival and movement of God down through history has begun as people have had courage to ask God to do more.

Obedience (vs 9-10)

You can't be intimate with Jesus and then live as you like. There is no loving him apart from obeying. Love and obedience go closely together. You can't say you love Jesus and then disobey his commands. If you love Jesus, then love will transpose itself into obedience; and if you obey Jesus then you are loving him. What has made life worth living? Living for yourself? Or that you have given yourself for others and that you have borne fruit?

The priority that Jesus reveals

Verse 8 is the central focus: 'This is to my Father's glory.' Not for our reputation but for his, to participate in his kingdom, and the spreading of his gospel. William Wilberforce was a man of remarkable capacity who played a major part around the time of Whitfield and Wesley, in restoring the evangelical faith to the land. He wrote a book of spirituality, and in it, in 1797, he says 'We no longer recognise the promotion of the glory of God and the possession of his favour as the object of our highest regard and most strenuous endeavour.' He says that 'we have avowedly established a system of decent selfishness. Recreation is our chief business, amusements multiply to fill up the void of a listless and languid life ... we are no longer motivated by the glory of the Father. We live to fill up the empty hours of our lives with selfishness, amusing ourselves, comforting ourselves, enjoying ourselves.'[3]

But the glory of God, as John Stott says, is the highest of all missionary motives.[4] We should go out with the gospel because we have a burning and passionate zeal for the glory of God. We are called to be, individually and corporately, a fruitful people, a fruitful community. Jesus says we are chosen and appointed to bear fruit, fruit that will last. What Israel failed to do, the church in this generation is called by divine and royal appointment to achieve. What will be your legacy as you review your life? Will anyone say you made a difference because you brought them the gospel? It's time to produce again in our land a spiritual harvest. Hear the call. God has chosen and appointed you to go and bear fruit that will last.

Endnotes

[1] Alistair Begg, *The Hand of God: Finding His Care in All Circumstances* (Chicago: Moody Press, 1999), p59.

[2] James 4:2.

[3] William Wilberforce, *Real Christianity* (Victor, 2005 edn. Org. 1797), p94f.

[4] John Stott, *The Message of Romans* (Nottingham: BST, IVP, 1994), p53.

A joyful community

by Peter Maiden

Peter Maiden

Keswick Ministries's current Chairman and International Director of Operation Mobilisation, Peter is a busy man! He travels extensively to fulfil his commitments with OM, overseeing the day-to-day co-ordination of its ministry in 106 countries worldwide. He is also an Elder of Hebron Evangelical Church in Carlisle, where he lives, and he manages to include itinerant Bible teaching in the UK and overseas into his schedule. Peter is married to Win, and they have three grown-up children and five grandchildren.

A joyful community

John 16

Introduction

One Sunday evening, in his diary, Robert Louis Stevenson gives the following comment; 'I went to church this morning and I wasn't depressed!' Obviously, his normal experience of church left him with depression and this was a wonderful exception. It reminds me of the tragic words of the poet Thomas Swinburne, 'Thou hast conquered, O pale Galilean. The world has grown grey because of Thee.' What an indictment of the church down through the centuries that we've managed to paint the Man who lived life most fully as a pale, insipid character.

The early church seemed to be rather different. We're told they found favour with all of the people (Acts 2:46), 'Every day they continued to meet together in the temple courts. They broke bread in their homes and ate together with glad and sincere hearts.' The church should be a community that attracts people through its infectious joy. Would you say that is the image that most people have of the church, in our nation today? Does that truly describe my church? Or your local church? For some, I'm sure the answer to that question would be 'Yes.' Thank God for that. For many, if we're honest, the answer is 'No.' But remember, if we answer that question with a 'No,' we *are* the church. And it may be that we're answering that question 'No' because our lives are not being transformed daily, by the joy of Christ.

Joy and peace in the middle of struggle

In John 16:22, Jesus says, 'Now is your time of grief, but I will see you again and you will rejoice, and no-one will take away your joy.' So there's the promise of joy. Then, verse 33, 'I've told you these things, so that in me you may have peace.' In chapter 15:18, Jesus promises his followers that they'll be hated by the world, just as he was. Persecution is promised (v20) and that opposition is specified in chapter 16:2. 'They will put you out of the synagogue,' Jesus said. Imagine what that would mean, in the deeply religious society where they were living. They would be completely ostracised. 'And' says Jesus, 'the feelings will be so intense that the time is coming when killing you will be seen to be a religious duty. If these people can catch you and kill you, that will be seen as a service offered to God.' Yet in the middle of all this, they're not just to keep their heads down and try to survive. Instead, Jesus calls his followers to carry on active witness (Jn. 15:26-27). Jesus says, 'When the Counsellor comes, whom I will send to you from the Father, the Spirit of truth who goes out from the Father, he will testify about me. And you also must testify . . .'

And he's going to leave them alone. He's going back to the One who sent him (Jn. 16:5). This announcement causes utter confusion and absolute uncertainty (vs 17–18). 'Some of his disciples said to one another, "What does he mean by saying, 'In a little while you will see me no more, and then after a little while, you will see me' and 'Because I'm going to the Father'?" They kept asking, "What does he mean by 'a little while'? We don't understand what he's saying."' You get the sense of sheer panic in those verses. So much to face and Jesus is not going to be there, it seems, to face it with them. And yet Jesus, quite remarkably, promises joy and peace in the middle of these days of violent uncertainty. I think we need to ask, don't we, 'How can I, how can we, the church, experience the joy of Jesus, even when, as must have been the case with the disciples, everything appears to be against us?' How can we experience, in the twenty first century, the joy of Jesus Christ?

What is joy?

I went to a local church, thousands of miles away from here. And when I got there, this church, obviously, by its practice, had a theology of total happiness. They believed you should be happy, if you're a Christian, 24/7. They expressed this by a sort of saintly smile over their faces. Every time you met them, they always had this saintly smile, which was very strange. It was even more strange, sitting in the congregation and watching the worship band, and watching a flautist, trying to play the flute with this saintly smile across her face. Certainly for me, the theology of total happiness worked because I enjoyed that fully. I laughed and laughed.

Joy is much more than an emotion, in Scripture. It's a spiritual quality, grounded upon God himself and it comes from our relationship with him. David writes '(God) you fill me with joy in your presence' (Ps. 16:11). Paul's famous exaltation to the Philippians says: 'Rejoice in the Lord always. I will say it again: Rejoice!' Joy is also one of the fruits born in our lives, through the ministry of the Holy Spirit. It is for me that deep underlying shalom peace; that deep sense of well being; the assurance that a sovereign God has his hand upon my life; that his Son has won eternal salvation for me; that there is no condemnation. I am in Christ Jesus. That's joy for me.

Remarkably, the Bible maintains that difficult experiences, sorrows and even the sort of persecution Jesus is speaking to his disciples about can actually enlarge our capacity for such joy. How can we know peace in the midst of these uncertainties? It's surely an urgent matter of witness that we, the body of Christ, experience more of this fruit and are able to display it to a watching world, through our lives. So I want to go through this passage and see what Jesus said should be the source of joy for his disciples, as he prepares to leave them, and should be the foundation of the joy in our lives today.

The character of Jesus

I see a wonderful tenderness, an immense sensitivity, in Jesus, in this passage, which gives me great hope and assurance. In verse 33, Jesus says, 'I have told you these things, so that in me you may have peace.' The things that he's just been telling them include the fact that they will forsake him.

Campbell Morgan comments, 'There is no peace so fine to the human soul, as the sense of realising that He knows me, even the worst that's in me.' Jesus knew that these disciples would soon forsake him. They would run for their lives. They would deny him. They would even doubt his resurrection. Yet he expresses his total commitment to them and, in a sense, his confidence in them. His confidence is only because of his commitment to them, his patience with them, but it's still there. He is saying, 'You're going to have trouble and in that trouble, initially, will be terrible denial, awful betrayal but take heart, I've overcome the world. I'm confident that ultimately you will be overcomers with me.'

Go back to verse 12: Jesus says, 'I have much more to say to you, more than you can now bear' and link that statement with verse 4. Jesus had just been explaining to them how they would be put out of the synagogue and even killed and then says 'I did not tell you this at first because I was with you.' Jesus only reveals things to us as we're able to bear the revelation. If the Lord Jesus had revealed everything that was going to happen to me, in advance, I would have run a mile. We've got a wonderful picture here of a tender Saviour, encouraging his followers. He knows they're weak but he's absolutely committed to seeing them through the rough times as well as the smooth. My Saviour and my friend, who I have the privilege to walk this world with.

How does he walk this world with us?

There's the second source of our joy. In verse 7, he makes this remarkable statement to his disciples: 'It is for your good that I am going away.' You can imagine their confusion, even their anger. 'You've just explained to us the struggles that we're about to face and now you're walking out on us. How can that possibly be to our advantage?' Maybe you've thought like that from time to time. But Jesus says to his disciples, 'It's for your good that I'm going.' Then he gives the reason. 'Unless I go away, the Counsellor will not come to you; but if I go, I will send him to you.' What does that mean?

Surely, it means two things Jesus is not saying, 'Two members of the Trinity can't be present with you at the same time.' All three are always present. As Bruce Milne puts it, 'Jesus is not talking so much about a spatial movement but a spiritual exaltation.'[1] Jesus must go away through death and resurrection to the glory of the Father's presence. Then, as he says, 'I'll send the Holy Spirit.' In sending the Holy Spirit, he will usher in the powers of the promised kingdom of God in the world.

Peter, in his address on the day of Pentecost, concentrated on that theme. Quoting the prophet Joel, he objected to the suggestion that the disciples were drunk. 'No, this is what was spoken by the prophet Joel: In the last days, God says, I will pour out my Spirit on all people.' That's how my Saviour, my Friend, walks with me and walks with you, through the dark times as well as the light times. He does so in the person of the Spirit.

The reality of the resurrection

The Holy Spirit, present with us now, assures us that we worship a resurrected Christ. We are people of the resurrection. It's the resurrected Jesus who has sent us the gift of his Holy Spirit.

In verse 16, Jesus says, 'In a little while you see me no more, and then after a little while you will see me.' What did he mean? Interpreters are divided over whether the 'little while' he's talking about refers to the age of the church and the seeing him after that refers to his glorious second coming. Or is he referring to them seeing him after his resurrection? I lean to the view that he's referring to his resurrection but both those statements are absolutely true.

In verse 22, he seems to be referring to his resurrection. 'Now is your time of grief, but I will see you again and you will rejoice, and no one can take away your joy.' How can we have such a joy and no power on earth take that joy from us? It's because that joy is based on events that have happened in history, that can never be reversed. Jesus is alive. He's defeated death and sin. The resurrection has set in motion a chain of events that no powers on earth can stop. In 1 Corinthians 15, Paul says 'Christ has been raised from the dead but that's only the beginning. He's the first fruits of those who have fallen asleep and all in Christ will be made alive and an order will follow. And if you want to know the order,' says Paul, 'I'll give it to you. Christ will be the first fruits. Then, when he comes, those who belong to him. Then the next step, in this now inevitable process, the end will come, when he hands over the kingdom to God the Father and God is all in all. The resurrection of Christ,' says Paul 'has sealed this.' There can be no turning back. A process has been set in motion which nothing and no one can thwart and it ends in final, glorious and complete victory.

There will be many struggles along the way. When I first wrote my notes, I put 'There may be many struggles' then I crossed it out. There *will* be many struggles along the way but the final victory is secure. Jesus says 'No one can take this joy away.' No one can take away this deep settled peace, which is often seen most clearly in times of intense struggle. Jesus has won the victory and the inevitable, unstoppable process is rolling forward and ends with God himself finally being all in all.

So many testimonies could be called upon to show that this is reality, not just theory. Richard Wurmbrand, that famous pastor who was imprisoned in Romania for so many years, spent many of those years in solitary confinement. After he was released, he wrote about his experiences and said something like this, 'They took everything from me but they couldn't take away my joy. I had to dance around the cell sometimes because I felt if I did not give my joy physical expression, somehow I would burst.' This is reality.

I got an e-mail this morning, from a friend of mine who works amongst the tribal people in Papua New Guinea. These people were totally without any knowledge of Jesus twenty years ago. Most of the tribe are now followers of Jesus and Jack said, 'One of these brothers was crushed yesterday morning by a falling tree. We could see he was on his way to heaven. He said to us "Jesus is waiting for me, it's my time to go." He asked for my New Testament. And then, after reading it for a little while, he laid it on his chest and died.'

Jesus has won the victory

I love the simplicity of the words of Jesus in verse 28. 'I came from the Father and entered the world; now I am leaving the world and going back to the Father.' It's almost a summary of his whole mission. 'I came from the Father' – his virgin birth, his incarnation. 'I entered the world' – his identification with us, his ministry amongst us. 'Now I am leaving the world and going back (by way of the cross) to the Father.' That phrase 'back to the Father' emphasises the victory. His statement of what will happen, step by step, is further evidence of his absolute control of the situation. As Jesus said, 'No one takes my life from me. I have the authority to lay it down and to take it up again. This authority, I received from my Father.' Our joy is that we know every-thing Jesus came to do, he did perfectly and completely. Our salvation has been perfectly, completely secured by his work. That's why Paul can write, 'There is now no condemnation for those who are in Christ Jesus.'

We have a constant relationship

But there's more, because while we run this race towards inevitable victory, achieved by the work of Christ, we have the joy of constant relationship with the Father, all along the way. Look at this fascinating statement (vs 26, 27); 'In that day you will ask in my name. I am not saying that I will ask the Father on your behalf. No, the Father him-self loves you.' Jesus is talking about a new, direct, intimate relationship with the Father. In the name of Jesus, we can enter the presence of the one who loves us. Jesus encourages us to do just that (v24): 'Until now you have not asked for anything in my name. Ask and you will receive, and your joy will be complete.' Up until this point, they'd brought their requests directly to Jesus. But, after his death and resurrection, everything would be different. By his death and resurrection, he would remove the barrier of sin. From then on, with utter confidence, they could address the Father directly through Jesus, knowing of the Father's love for them.

The Father speaks direct to us

Not only can we speak directly to the Father, he speaks to us. In verse 13, Jesus promises his disciples, 'When . . . the Spirit of truth comes, he will guide you into all truth.' This was to be one of the special ministries of the Holy Spirit. It's a promise we must apply primarily to the apostles and the books of the New Testament are the result of this promise. It's the promise of special, unique inspiration for the apostles to deliver the New Testament Scriptures to the people of God. Through all the ups and downs of life, as we move towards the inevitable victory of our Lord Jesus, we have this wonderful constant companionship of the Holy Spirit, using the Scriptures to reveal more and more of the majesty of our God to us.

Is there any reason we should not be a community of joy and our local churches known, within the community, as places of joy? We need to be very real about the struggles. Living for Christ in this age – in any age – involves real struggle. We don't want to be less than honest about those struggles. I don't have all the answers to the issues of even my life, never mind the lives of the hundreds of people I have the privilege of speaking to. Many things that happen in and around my life and the lives of my friends, I can't understand and I can't adequately explain. The last thing I'm appealing for is a sort of mindless triumphalism. But, although we cannot immediately understand or explain everything, I have, and I trust you have, this deep down conviction that, one day, we shall understand these things. Because our sovereign God reigns and we know his Son to be a tender Saviour and Shepherd, who has taken on all our enemies and solidly defeated them, as seen by his resurrection. That resurrection set in motion a train of events which are unstoppable and will lead to the ultimate reign of Christ, in the home of righteousness, and the knowledge of those realities is surely the key to our joy.

I read an article, three weeks ago, written by a Christian man who attended two meetings in one day. He wrote that the first meeting was rather like a strategy meeting in the culture war.

> Participants were discussing such things as the decline of marriage, the destruction of unborn human beings, the flattening of human sexuality into contextless pleasure and so on. All were earnestly committed to the causes and most, to be blunt, were not having a good time. I support many if not all of their aims. There is a time for concerted action, forceful advocacy, when a culture is beset, as ours indisputably is, with violence against the weak and the disintegration of our deepest promises. But then there was violence and disintegration in the day of Jesus too and Jesus was hardly shy about confronting the patterns of sin, in his culture, though he was consistently harder on the pious than he was on the pagans. But everywhere Jesus went, life blossomed. The sick were healed, lepers were touched, daughters and sons were plucked from the mouth of the grave. Jesus left behind him a trail of leaps and laughter. Reunited families, terrific wine, as well as dumbfounded synagogue leaders, uneasy monarchs and sleepless procurators. His witness against violence, amidst a culture in rebellion against the good, was neither withdrawal nor war. It was simply life, abundant, generous, just life; and ultimately a willingness to let the enemies of life do their worst, confident that even death could not extinguish the abundant life of God. Many of the people in that room wore countenances etched with some combination of depression and derision. It's hard to believe someone who speaks of love through clenched teeth.

Then the writer moved on to a second meeting.

> It took place in a cosy living room, furnished with well worn sofas. Kentucky fried was on the menu and a few candles were flickering. The leaders were laughing, talking, catching up on one another's stories. All

kinds of people, from all kinds of backgrounds, drawn to one another by the gospel. The conversation died down, prayer began. We soaked in a comforting, empowering silence. Then we talked about the church's abundance of ministries, shortage of finance, the dizzying array of needs to be found just by going a few streets in any direction and the biblical stories of God's people in exile. Agents of peace in the midst of pagan cities. I felt, that night, a feeling of tremendous hope. The hope I find, over and over again, in the most unlikely places; in war zones, both figurative and literal, where Christ's followers worship and serve.

Nothing can break your heart quite like the church but neither is there anything that can so restore your heart as being among just a few people whose love is transparent, tenacious and utterly not their own doing.

The writer finished the article by saying this

> I don't know how or whether the culture war can ever be won. Human culture, like human nature, is too intractable for unambiguous victories. I suspect we've consigned our armies to a conflict that's unwinnable by definition and by making disciples into warriors, we've risked robbing them of the hilarious high calling that is the birth right of every Christian; to be an agent of improbable, impossible life, in the midst of a dark world.

I have to say that I sometimes detect something similar to that in Bible expositions. It's vital to rightly divide the word of truth. But sometimes excellent Bible expositions leave me sad and disappointed. The exposition may be absolutely accurate and sound, biblically, but it's not delivered in a spirit of generosity. Those who don't agree with the expositor, on every small detail, can be harshly dealt with. I come away from some of those expositions feeling, 'There's not much joy and generosity around.' That's the calling of the church; to be a joyful, generous, community, in the midst of this fallen world.

Satan is a brilliant thief. He loves to rob us of the joy that Jesus died to purchase for us. It's the great joy robbery. If you're sitting there tonight thinking, 'I've lost my joy,' I hope you'll do something about it, because our joy is based on historical and present realities. It's a gift for every one of God's people. You may be going through some deep emotional issue and right now you just can't quite embrace that truth and that's understandable. Hang in there and God will see you through. Some of you would say 'For years I've lost my joy.' It's been robbed by the great thief, Satan himself. You're not embracing truth and you may even be beginning to believe the enemy's lies. Embrace these truths and you'll regain those possessions which Christ went to the cross to purchase for us. A community of joy; the church.

Endnotes

[1] Bruce Milne, *The Message of John* (IVP: BST series, Nottingham, 1993).

Flawed heroes – Judges

Deborah – an iron lady

by Derek Tidball

Judges 4–5

Introduction

I was about eight years old when my mother was taken ill. A very pious elder from our local Brethren assembly came to visit her. He looked at my mother and said, 'Joan, you're a real mother in Israel, you know.' I didn't have a clue what he was talking about. This sounded a wonderfully pious expression, 'mother in Israel'; but she only had two children, not a whole tribe. Years later, I discovered that this is what Deborah calls herself in Judges chapter 5, where she says, 'Villagers in Israel would not fight until I arose a mother in Israel.'[1] I was left even more puzzled by what the elder of the Brethren Assembly meant, when he applied this great phrase of Deborah to my mother.

The phrase you have in the title of the Keswick programme for this address is 'Deborah – an iron lady.' I assure you my mother was not an iron lady. And I want you to disabuse yourself of that phrase, to some extent, because immediately into your mind comes Mrs Thatcher and all that she stood for. We can easily project her image onto Deborah, rather than letting the word of God speak for itself.

We tend to read Judges 4 and 5 as the story of Deborah. But it is not so much about Deborah as about God. He choreographs the whole sequence of events that is going on here. In Judges chapter 4, God is mentioned seven times. When the perfect number seven arises about God, we need to sit up and take notice.

The discipline of the Lord (vs 1-4)

Deserved discipline

You'll know the cycle of events that takes place in Judges: how the children of Israel get into a position of idolatry and unbelief and God steps in to discipline them. After a period of time, they turn to God and cry out to him in anguish. Then God, in his grace, sends them a judge or deliverer and, under that deliverer, they know both freedom from oppression and freedom to follow in his ways. But, as time goes on, they grow unfaithful and distant from God again.

Chapter 4 of Judges begins way down in the valley. 'Again the Israelites did evil in the eyes of the LORD, now that Ehud was dead.' So God moved against them in discipline. It was a deserved discipline. The restraint of Ehud, the previous judge, had been removed. Without his firm grip on the situation, they went back to their old ways. In reading Judges, time and time again you want to cry out 'When will they ever learn?' But then we know how in our own lives God teaches us a lesson and we think we have got on top of it and then, as time goes on, we fall back into our old ways.

God's discipline here is neither random nor undeserved. It's not that God woke up, as other gods in the ancient world might have done, with a headache and decided to throw a thunderbolt at Israel. His discipline is always a discipline which is just and deserved.

Severe discipline

On this occasion, it was not only deserved but it was also severe, in many ways. The enemy that now moved against the tribes of Israel was the powerful enemy of Canaan, the name of the local inhabitants. This was the third group of people who had caused problems for Israel. Earlier in Judges, the people of Cushan-Rishathaim (3:8) had caused trouble. And then the children of Moab, to the south east of Israel (3:12) had moved against them.

This was serial opposition. Each time it got more serious and on this occasion, the enemy that God uses to exercise his discipline is the powerful people of Canaan. We know that they are powerful, for they are at the leading technological edge of their day. They have nine hundred chariots fitted with iron. Iron was becoming the key metal and it's being turned, already, into an instrument of warfare. In Deborah's day, they greeted the opposition of these Canaanites with their nine hundred chariots of iron with horror, for they were far more powerful weapons than those Israel could respond with. So overwhelming was their military technology that Israel didn't have a hope.

God's discipline was also severe because it lasted twenty years.

Effective discipline

But God's discipline was also effective. For, when they reached their lowest ebb, they cried to the Lord. The discipline is not being exercised for the sake of retribution. It is there in order to provoke a change of behaviour, to transform a heart, to move people back to God. It is effective for it doesn't cause them to rebel further but rather invites them to renew their relationship with God. It's there to persuade them to live better and to restore their broken covenant relationship with God. Would that all discipline were so motivated and that all discipline were that effective.

We tend not to think too much of the discipline of the Lord in our Christian lives. We think, 'That's old covenant.' But the New Testament speaks about the Lord disciplining his people, very explicitly, on at least two occasions. Paul rebukes the Corinthians for their behaviour at the Lord's table in 1 Corinthians 11 and says to them, 'Some of you are weak and ill and have fallen asleep because you have eaten and drunk the body and the blood of Christ in an unworthy manner.' In other words, God has moved against your misbehaviour in the church, in discipline.

The other great passage about discipline is found in Hebrews 12:4-13, where the author reminds us that it is a sign of God's love. God disciplines us in a whole variety of ways; sometimes through direct circumstances, but often through indirect circumstances, by what's happening around us in life, as in the case of the Canaanites here, moving against Israel. I wonder if it's effective in moving us back to God. We are so anxious these days to disconnect sin from suffering and indeed Jesus disconnects them in Luke 13:1-5: 'Why did the tower fall on people in Siloam, was it because they sinned worse than others? No, it happened for other reasons.' There isn't always a direct cause and effect connection between sin and suffering. But, in our eagerness to affirm this and disconnect them, maybe we don't now have a place for the discipline of the Lord at all.

What is it in the circumstances in your life that might be a messenger from God to say that you're not following him as closely and as faithfully as you should? Can you trace God's discipline in your life and if so, how do you react to it? Do you even acknowledge it as from the Lord and if you do, do you react with anger and resentment or with gratitude, because it's an invitation to return to him?

Charles Spurgeon once said that

> I'm afraid that all the grace I have gotten out of my comfortable and easy times and happy hours, almost lies on a penny [they're virtually nothing in their extent]. But the good that I have received from my sorrows and pains and griefs is all together incalculable. What do I not owe to the hammer and the anvil, the fire and the file? Affliction is the best bit of furniture in my house.[2]

What place have you for the discipline of the Lord?

The instrument of the Lord (vs 5-7,10)

We're introduced to Deborah; this amazing, unusual judge. She's introduced in verses 4 through to 7. In chapter 5:8, we further read that God chose new leaders

> when war came to the city gates,
> but not a shield or spear was seen
> among forty thousand in Israel.

Among those leaders was Deborah. She did not set herself up in leadership. She was in leadership in response to the call of God. Many male Bible commentators look at this and say, 'Deborah was only chosen because the men weren't doing what they were supposed to be doing.' But we ought not to read into Scripture what is not there and there is no hint here that that was the situation. Deborah was chosen, in her own right, because of her spiritual qualities.

Her family situation

Deborah was not only a woman in leadership but a married woman in leadership. We know nothing about whether she had children or a family but that's a likely assumption. We know nothing about her husband, Lappidoth, other than his name. He was the also-ran, the husband who walked three or four steps behind his wife, who was the leader. Perhaps he was a nonentity. Who can tell? God, quite frankly, doesn't seem to have a problem, either here or elsewhere, with women in leadership.

Her leadership record

Verse 4: 'Deborah, a prophetess . . . was leading Israel at that time.' She sat under a particular palm tree and people would bring their civil cases, their disputes, and their community issues to her there, for her to exercise judgement. They knew where she would be found. She was a woman of wisdom and discernment and had proved herself in many difficult situations.

They practised, in those days, something much more akin to our civil law than our criminal law. It was much less developed than our justice system: theirs was not an impersonal state. But Deborah took the responsibility, because of the call of God, to lead the children of Israel. And her track record equipped her to be trusted in a crisis, so when war came they looked to her and depended on her. It's important to realise that it was not the war that made her the leader. Often in history we have that discussion about Churchill; would he have been a great leader or was it the war that made him the leader? With Deborah there is no doubt, she had a proven track record as judge and as leader in her community before the war situation arose.

Here is a spiritual lesson for those who are younger leaders. Before God will trust you with great things, you need to learn to serve him in the lesser things. In order that you might be trusted with much, you must prove yourself with little. Jesus makes it very clear that God won't trust you with spiritual things, if you've proved unfaithful with material things. God won't trust you to great leadership, if you can't be trusted with small leadership issues first.[3]

As a Bible college principal, to illustrate, it matters to me how my students treat the books in the library. Sometimes students are known to take library books out, without registering them so they get lost or, even better, they creatively reshelve the library books so that they can find them and nobody else can! If they can't be trusted with handling the library books, which are material things, why on earth is God going to trust them with the church? If you can't be trusted with the small, why is God going to trust you with the great?

Her spiritual sensitivity

Deborah had proved herself before the crisis situation arose when God communicated with her in a direct way. Revelation came to her, about the situation she faced, the circumstances Israel was in. She was receptive and open and sensitive to the words of God. She's not the only female prophet in the Old Testament. There's Huldah, who plays a significant part much later in Israel's history.[4] God sometimes uses the unconventional, the surprising person because they're less busy and more open, more sensitive, to him. We need prophets who will hear God's contemporary word for today's church and pass it on as faithfully as Deborah did.

Her active commitment

She proved herself to be a leader because she was not lethargic or indifferent to the plight of Israel. Right through this chapter, there are notes about geography. Geography matters here. Deborah exercised her leadership between Ramah and Bethel: she lived in the very south of the country. When trouble arose from the Canaanites, it was in the far north of the country, around the foot of Mount Carmel. She could have said, 'That's for the northern tribes to sort out, not for me. We're all right down here.' But what makes a leader is that they are determined to do something about the situation, rather than let the situation just go on. They are going to get involved rather than remain apathetically uninvolved.

I don't know whether you know the story of Bear Grylls. He is a Christian who was in the British army and broke his back when he jumped out of a plane and had a parachute accident while he was serving in Africa. He was determined to get fit and overcome that disability. Subsequently he became the youngest Briton ever to climb to the top of Everest and descend again alive. Younger people have gone up there but not got back. He's written about his experiences in his book *Facing Up.*[5]

Listening to him lecture last year at an event for the Shaftesbury Society at Harrow School, he began by asking, 'What is the difference between the extraordinary and the ordinary? It is the word "extra."' What makes a leader? What makes somebody stand out from the ordinary, is that they take on board the extra. The ordinary person will sit there saying, 'Awfully bad news from up north. Isn't it a shame?' Deborah, hearing the word of the Lord, goes that extra mile and takes action. It's a key quality of leadership.

J. Oswald Saunders, in that classic book on spiritual leadership from some years ago, says, 'The young person of leadership calibre will work while others waste time, study while others sleep, pray while others play.'[6] If you want to be in leadership, there's a cost to be paid. It doesn't just happen but it does happen to the Deborahs of this world for she got up out of her armchair and took an initiative, and did something about the need in the north.

Contrast that with Barak, whom she asks to lead the troops (v8). Barak says to her, 'If you go with me, I will go but if you don't go with me, I won't go.' It's not quite clear how we are to interpret that verse. Some people like Michael Wilcock say that it is a good thing. Barak is saying, in all humility, 'You are the focus of God's blessing, Deborah, and if I'm going into battle, I want you there because I want God's blessing right with me at the side.' More usually, people say, 'Come on, Barak, be a man. Why do you need a woman at your side to go into battle? This is a lack of faith. This is lethargy on your part. You're lacking courage.' It's difficult to be sure how to interpret it.

Whether Barak was hesitating or not, Deborah showed no hesitation. That's one of the themes to develop out of these chapters. When you go into chapter 5, to the song of victory that Deborah composes after the battle, she ranges over the tribes of Israel. She compliments a number of tribes for getting into the action and fighting with the northern tribes but she also rebukes a number of tribes. 'Oh, in Reuben' she says, 'there was much searching of heart.' They never actually did anything but oh, did they perspire: 'Should we get involved? Isn't it dreadful?' The action was all over before they ever got off their behinds and did anything about it. Gilead stayed safely behind, beyond the Jordan. Dan lingered by their ships, Asher stayed in their caves. Probably that was a safe place to be just in case any of these iron chariots came anywhere near them. Deborah is distinguished as an iron lady, against the iron chariots; a woman of action.

The foresight of the Lord

The foreknowledge and the sovereignty of God is remarkably clear in this chapter. There are two outstanding examples of God's foresight and God's providential planning that come up. The first is in respect of Barak (v9) and the second in respect of Heber (v11).

When Barak says, 'I'll only go if you come with me, Deborah,' Deborah replies 'Because of the course you are taking, the honour of victory will not be yours, for the LORD will deliver Sisera into the hands of woman.' That's probably the best reason for assuming that when Barak says, 'I won't go unless you come with me,' it's a lack of faith on Barak's part. God says, through Deborah the prophet, 'That's fine but the honour of victory will come through a woman.' But that woman is not Deborah but Jael. There is poor Barak, sandwiched between these two women; Deborah and Jael. Two women who are willing, eager instruments of God, at either end, and a man who is at least hesitant, in the middle.

God has his plan and insures that Barak will not say at the end, 'The victory was mine really, it was the circumstances. I was just unfortunate that I wasn't there at the final kill, but I got the victory.' No. God knows exactly what's going to happen and says, 'You play your part, Barak, and it will be a significant part but the honour of victory will go to Jael, a woman.'

And the foresight of God is seen, not only in respect of Barak in verse 9, but also in respect of Heber in verse 11. This is one of these verses that sound like geography. You tend to look at these details and think, 'What's that all about?' 'Heber the Kenite had left the other Kenites, the descendants of Hobab, Moses's brother-in-law, and pitched his tent by the great tree at Zaanannim near Kadesh.' God is actually moving his people into place, long before he needs to. Here is this non-pure Jew, this person from outside of the twelve tribes; the Kenite, whom God is positioning so that, at the right moment, when Jael needs to be ready, he's got her in the right place to achieve the victory.

I remember Donald Guthrie, who was our vice principal, expounding the story of Philip and the Ethiopian eunuch and remarking on the sheer wonder of how it was that God, in his sovereignty, arranged for Philip the evangelist, who was having a successful evangelistic campaign in Samaria, to go into the desert and meet, at exactly the right moment, the Ethiopian eunuch, who was returning home from Jerusalem. It truly is a remarkable conjunction of circumstances. Such is the sovereignty of God in our lives as so often he moves people into place and demonstrates that he's the one in charge.

The triumph of God (vs 12–23)

The victory is in two parts: the victory of Barak and then the final victory of Jael from verse 12 onwards. As the scholars have looked at these verses, they've tried to analyse them as a literary structure. Often a chapter or a part of Scripture is written with a structure and what starts at the beginning is complemented by how it ends and so it moves through, phrase by phrase complementing each other, until you get to a single point in the middle, a sort of arrow head. That point is the key lesson. When people have done a literary structure analysis of this chapter, the point of the arrow head – the key to these structures – is verse 14. Look at what it says: 'Deborah said to Barak, "Go, this is the day the LORD has given Sisera into your hands. Has not the LORD God gone ahead of you? Victory belongs to the LORD."'

As in many of the films, *The Lord of the Rings* and *Alexander* and all the others, you get these magnificent cinematic effects of the king at the front of the army, leading the troops out to certain victory. Here we have the Lord of hosts, the sovereign Lord of the universe, going ahead of Barak, to ensure certain victory.

On the battlefield with Barak (vs 14-16)

They meet in the river bed of Kishon which is usually a dry wadi most of the time and certainly at this time of the year. So Sisera, the hostile captain, confidently takes his nine hundred chariots of iron into that situation. He'd have never done so, of course, unless he was sure that he was going to be successful and the outcome was going to go his way. But then as he takes his chariots into this dry river bed, God opens up the heavens and a miraculous downpour occurs. So the river bed, which had been parched, suddenly becomes a muddy swamp. The flash flood captures these iron chariots and bogs them down. The very technology that they had boasted of actually now becomes a liability.

> When you LORD went out from Seir,
> when you marched from the land of Edom,
> the earth shook, the heavens poured
> the clouds poured down water (Judg. 5:4).

> The river Kishon swept them away,
> the age old river, the river Kishon,
> march on my soul, be strong (Judg. 5:21).

Sisera would never have been foolish enough to have sent his troops into such an unwise situation. He knew that it was safe to send those nine hundred chariots into that situation; but God had a better plan. In the middle of a heat wave, sudden downpours take place that can wash bridges away or flood whole towns, as happened in Cornwall the summer before last. This isn't poppycock, this isn't fantasy, this is reality. The miraculous thing is the timing of it.

In the bedroom with Jael (v17–22)

God stopped Sisera's chariots in their tracks and his army was defeated but he fled. He ends up where Heber the Kenite had planted his tent (v11), being offered hospitality by Jael, his wife, as he flees on his way back home to Jabin the king. She invites him in, gives him hospitality, puts him to sleep. He's exhausted by now. She lays him down, covers him over, in order that he might recover his strength. Then, in one of the most graphic and bloodthirsty bits of the Old Testament, she picks up a tent peg and bangs it through his temple and kills him.

There are a number of things you need to understand about this. First of all, women erected the tents in those days. So when she was wielding the hammer to bang in the tent peg, she knew what she was doing. That was women's work, not men's work. Secondly, you think, 'Isn't she betraying the trust that she'd displayed by offering Sisera such hospitality?' It could be that that's what she's doing. But it could be that she didn't recognise who Sisera was until she'd given him the drink and laid him down to sleep. Thirdly, you might want to say, 'Isn't this an immoral act of God? Surely we don't believe in a God who would do this sort of thing?'

As one Old Testament commentator Dale Ralph Davis points out, she didn't ask that question, so popular today, 'What would Jesus do?' for she lived before she could 'enjoy such light.'[7] And, truth to tell, that often leads us to a sentimental reaction. I'm not always sure Jesus would respond in the way in which we sometimes answer that question.

Here's the revelation of a God of justice on behalf of his people who are desperate and in need of defence. Here is an enemy who would certainly not have spared any of the Israelites. Whether the Bible seems to approve of the action or not, here we see the principles that God's people need to challenge evil, and that God is on the side of the oppressed and the poor. Israel didn't have nine hundred chariots to respond to Sisera's army. They were the underdogs and God has his strategy for bringing those underdogs and making them, as it were, over dogs. With the hindsight of history, we look back at a number of people like Bonhoeffer, who joined in the plot to assassinate Hitler at the end of the Second World War, and we treat them as heroes. We should treat Jael with no less honour.

Maybe the response Jael makes is like using poison. Poison is always poison and poison is always dangerous. But sometimes, in medicine, poison has a useful place, in fighting a greater enemy, a worse disease. Although poison always remains poison, sometimes it can be a necessary medicine.

What does all this say to you and me today?

As individual believers

We need to be wary of claiming 'The Lord is on our side' in all our personal battles. This was about God keeping his covenant promise to Israel, no matter how much they went off the rails. We need to be a people who ask, 'Where are the signs of God's discipline in our lives? Where are we straying from the Lord? Where are we in God's greater salvation story?' Yet surely, too, we can derive encouragement from the Lord going ahead of us, as he did the armies of Israel.

As leaders

There are plenty of leadership lessons from Deborah concerning the need to be sensitive to God's word, to be ready for action at any time and not hanging back while we say to others, 'After you.'

As the church today

We need to wake up because, though we are very active, we seem so feeble and powerless. The church does seem to be in a period of oppression. Maybe we should, like the children of Israel, cry out to the Lord for help. We're so regularly turning to human strategies, perhaps we're not desperate enough and so not crying out to the Lord enough.

To all of us

Here is a call not to be indifferent to injustice but to get involved and to fight for righteousness. Not with the weapons that Barak and Jael used. Not with literal violence. But with all the spiritual armoury which is available to us: the weapons of the new covenant. We need to use every gift we have for the benefit of the wider society, in this democratic country of ours; getting stuck in to the public debates about morality and law and social good and trying to establish the gospel again in our nation. Then the Lord will go before us. The Lord will give us, in his own good time, the Deborahs to lead us.

Endnotes

[1] The version of the Bible used here is Today's New International Version.

[2] This quote from C. H. Spurgeon is not infrequently used, though the original source of it is now untraceable.

[3] Luke 16:10-12.

[4] 2 Kings 22:14; 2 Chronicles 34:22.

[5] Bear Grylls, *Facing Up* (London: Macmillan, 2000).

[6] J. Oswald Sanders, *Spiritual Leadership* (Lakeland, 1967), p45.

[7] Dale Ralph Davis, *Judges: Such a Great Salvation* (Nairn: Christian Focus Books, 2000), p78.

Jephthah – a foolish promise

by Dave Fenton

Dave Fenton

A native man of Kent, converted at college where he met his wife Heather, Dave now works for Keswick Ministries as the Director of Programming, which includes the delivery of Root 66 courses for youth and children's workers all over the UK. He has led the youth team at Keswick for many years and was Youth and Children's Co-ordinator at Christ Church, Fulwood. In his other life, Dave is Associate Pastor at Christ Church, Winchester. His marriage to Heather has produced three wonderful sons, three wonderful daughters-in-law and four wonderful grandsons.

Jephthah – a foolish promise

Judges 10: 17 – 12:7

Introduction

Before we get into the detail of the story, one of the important things to understand when we read the Bible is the context that we read it in and the understanding of that in a story like this is absolutely vital. From the Fall in Genesis 3 through to the arrival of Jesus, the one thing that runs right through the Bible is God's passion to save his people: 'salvation history'. God is in the business of saving his people. The covenant promise he made to Abraham in Genesis 12 is that God's people would be in God's land to enjoy his blessing and be under his rule. And if that's out of kilter in any way, God is in the business of restoration, of bringing back.

This particular story comes in the context of God still doing that, of restoring his people to their rightful place. At the end of chapter 10, we read that things are looking less than good. At this time in Israel's history, tribal bush wars were breaking out all over the place. They were a constant source of problem to Israel. The tribes were quite small, city-state tribes, all the 'ites' that you read about in the Bible, the Ammonites, the Amorites, the Moabites, the Edomites. They were an absolute menace to Israel, a constant thorn in Israel's side. Then 'the Ammonites were called to arms and camped in Gilead'

(10:17). There was a threat to God's precious chosen people, who were seeking to move into the land that God had promised them, trying to be God's people in the place that God had chosen, to obey his rule and to live under his blessing. All that was under threat, because the Ammonites, a tribe who were aggressive towards God's people, were camped in Gilead.

The Ammonites were ready to pounce. They were assembled and there was not a lot of Israelite leadership around to deal with it. 'The leaders of the people of Gilead said to each other, "Whoever will launch the attack against the Ammonites will be the head of all those living in Gilead."' It's like one of those fairy stories: 'If you're a good boy, you can have the kingdom.' If you're God's people, shouldn't there have been a strategic plan in place? But they simply weren't prepared to deal with attacks from the evil one.

There are Christians around like that. We need, as God's people, to be aware that camped around us are people who threaten what we believe. Some people solve that by diving into almost monastic Christianity: churches with their drawbridges up. How many churches do you know where the drawbridges are up? The reason is, we haven't learnt how to deal with people who come in with loads of baggage which is not Christian.

They weren't ready for it. 'The leaders of the people of Gilead said to each other "Whoever will launch the attack against the Ammonites will be the head of all those living in Gilead."' That's very tempting, isn't it, all that prestige, but it means that there is not a clear plan or the strength and probably the will to resist the threat.

Here is a common theme in the Old Testament, that cry of 'Where is the Saviour?' That comes over and over again: I'd love to take you through a quick Bible overview. Think of the number of times in salvation history when God sends a saviour figure. There is a circle of Old Testament tragedy which goes round and round. The people do all kinds of things, God sends someone to speak truth and judgement to them, the people repent and, for a bit, live as God intended them to live. Then they go back on themselves and it goes round and round until we get to the prophetic era and we find there the cry 'Where is the one who will come?' And then we see John the Baptist announce that there was one coming whose sandals he was not worthy to untie. Who will save the people from their sin?

Once the Fall has come, God has to act to bring his people salvation. All the way through the Old Testament he's saying, 'This is something which I need you to be aware of. I want you to see coming, finally and completely, the once for all sacrifice of Jesus on the cross.' Here we get it prefigured in Judges. It comes up over and over again in the Old Testament. The Passover is another obvious one. Just think of all the examples of God sending saviour figures.

The unlikely hero (Judges 11:1-3)

Verse 1: 'Jephthah the Gileadite was a mighty warrior.' We need one of them because we've got a mob camped outside: useful credentials for the current crisis. But he's not quite right. He doesn't come from the right stock. This man has clearly been – how can I put it? Despised and rejected by men? 'His father was Gilead; his mother was a prostitute' (v1). Surely not good salvation credentials. But this man, despised and rejected, was going to be the saviour of God's people. Does that ring a few bells? The man Christ Jesus whom, Peter said to the people, 'you crucified . . . God raised from the dead.' The rejected man of the people is the Saviour of the people. He was qualified but he didn't fit into the establishment.

Gilead had an affair with a prostitute and Jephthah was the result. Later Gilead had legitimate sons and family economics creep in. 'You are not going to get any inheritance in our family because you are the son of another woman.' Jephthah was kicked out because he was an embarrassment to the family reputation: a remnant of an unfortunate night of passion, something Gilead wanted to forget.

This rings a few bells to me. Quite famous people in our country, who get up to things they shouldn't, then don't want to take the consequences for their actions and say, 'My private life is nobody's business.' But if you're in a position of responsibility, it is our business and you can't just absolve yourself of responsibility by saying, 'My private life is my affair.'

There's not many places for such a man to go so he ends up in an extremely dodgy place (v3): 'Jephthah fled from his brothers and settled in the land of Tob where a group of adventurers gathered around him and followed him.' Dale Ralph Davis, whose commentary I've spent a lot of time working with, describes them as 'a band of free-booting guerrillas led by a social outcast.'[1] It was not an aristocratic Jewish resort, it was a place for society's dregs and thugs. That is where Jephthah lived.

Parallels (vs 1-11)

This was not the first time that God's people had cried out for help and there are parallels running between the two chapters. Chapter 10:10

> Then the Israelites cried out to the LORD, 'We have sinned against you, forsaking our God and serving the Baals.' The LORD replied, 'When the Egyptians, the Amorites, the Ammonites, the Philistines, the Sidonians, the Amalekites and the Maonites oppressed you and you cried to me for help, did I not save you from their hands? But you have forsaken me and served other gods, so I will no longer save you. Go and cry out to the gods you have chosen. Let them save you when you are in trouble!'

The people were in trouble in a previous event; they cried out, 'God, help! Please will you help us?' And Yahweh said, 'Hang on a bit. I delivered you. I saved you. I brought you out of Egypt. I parted the Red Sea for you. I did all those things for you, and as soon as you get out of it, you start moaning, and you start saying "We've got lots of other great gods now, that's brilliant!" And God says, "Why should I help you?"' Look at the parallel here (11:4–7). The Ammonites made war on Israel, the elders go to Jephthah and Jephthah replies, 'Didn't you hate me and drive me from my father's house? Why do you come to me now ...?' It's exactly parallel. Why should God respond? 'I saved you, I was a deliverer. In easier times, you forget I exist.' But they still go to Jephthah when they're in a jam.

Read the history of Israel and look at the number of times that God's people forgot him in times of ease. It's very possible for us to do exactly the same. What kind of relationship is that? If I need a clean shirt and say to my wife, 'Darling, I need a clean shirt. I don't care what you do for the rest of the day, just make sure my shirt's clean when I need it' – what kind of husband would I be if I did that?

That's the way we often are with God. We cry out when we're stuck. And God says, 'That isn't how I want you to be. I am the God of Israel. You are my people. I want a relationship with you and I want it every day, through all the changing scenes of life. I want it in the joys and the sorrows . . . I want you to know that I'm your God.'

The men of Gilead go to Jephthah only when they're in a jam, when the land is threatened. It's so parallel with God's words in 10:14, 'Why should I save God's people?' There's a New Testament parallel here. Wicked men put Jesus to death and Peter's appeal to the people (Acts 2:23) to repent and be baptised: 'It's in the name of Christ who was rejected that you can be saved.' God is going to do it. God is going to save by using a prostitute's son who was a family reject. His training ground in Tob would help him no end because he was a street fighter, a tough guy, streetwise. God says, 'That's my man!' I think we've prescribed the kind of guys we like to become Christians: quiet, respectable, nice people. If we get a guy who's a bit of a street fighter, we don't like people like that. God forgive us.

The battle is joined (11:12–28)

'. . . Jephthah sent messengers to the Ammonite king with the question: "What do you have against us that you have attacked our country?"' He's simply saying, 'What's the problem? Let's talk about it.' The problem goes back to the Exodus, the movement through the lands that God's people had to do in journeying from Egypt up to the Promised Land. Israel apparently stole land that belonged to Ammon. Ammon wants it back and want it peaceably, initially (v13). Jephthah puts a good case (vs 17–19).

Then Israel sent messengers to the king of Edom, saying, 'Give us permission to go through your country,' but the king of Edom would not listen. They sent also to the king of Moab, and he refused. So Israel stayed at Kadesh. Next they travelled through the desert, skirted the lands of Edom and Moab, passed along the eastern side of the country of Moab, and camped on the other side of the Arnon. They did not enter the territory of Moab, for the Arnon was its border.

They tried to keep the peace. Six hundred thousand people trampling through your land is not good news. A similar process was adopted with the next group, the Amorites (vs 19–20): 'Then Israel sent messengers to Sihon king of the Amorites, who ruled in Heshbon, and said to him, "Let us pass through your country to our own place." Sihon, however, did not trust Israel to pass through his territory. He mustered all his men and encamped at Jahaz and fought with Israel.'

People often say how vindictive and cruel God is in the Old Testament. But God does not just zap people when he feels like it. These people had consistently been a thorn in the side of Israel. Isn't it amazing how people twist the truth slightly? That's what the Ammonites had done: they'd said, 'This is our land.' Jephthah said, 'No. Moab and Edom we avoided. Ammon, you were never there; that was Amorite land. Yes, we did conquer it because the people came against us. God delivered us from the hand of the Amorites. It was never your land.' And just to add to their injury, he says, 'Why don't you go to your god, Chemosh, and ask him to get you some land? Our God has given us his land and this, mate, is not yours. So get out of here.' That's roughly what it says, that's a fairly free translation!

Commentators have found a problem here because Chemosh is not the god of Ammon; Chemosh is the god of Moab. Milcom was the god of Ammon. But Chemosh was a god acknowledged way beyond Moab. Jephthah argues (v26), 'For three hundred years Israel occupied Heshbon, Aroer, the surrounding settlements and all the towns along the Arnon. Why didn't you retake them during that time?'

Jephthah has painted a picture of God's salvation. 'He brought us up out of the land of Egypt. We wandered around in the desert and did all sorts of silly things that we shouldn't have done but God did what he promised. We try to keep good relationships but if people come up against us, and say, "No, this isn't yours and we're going to beat you up!" then God intervenes.' God says, 'I will protect my people' and if people rise up against God's people, they take the consequences for that and that's what happened when Sihon, king of the Amorites, raised an army against God's people. God is not mocked. God is Sovereign: he knows what he's doing and why he's doing it. And if people stand against the will of God, God will deal with them, in his own way. God was going to deal with the Ammonites.

'The king of Ammon, however, paid no attention to the message Jephthah sent him.' He ignored it and people that ignore God speaking to them must take the consequences. Isn't that the message of the gospel? The gospel is there, it's open, it's free. But if you ignore what it says, you will suffer for it. The Ammonites are defeated (vs 29–32): God gives the Ammonites into the hands of Jephthah. But in the midst of this there's a very big twist: Jephthah makes this vow.

This seems to be a perfect story – God has made this happen, the Ammonites have been defeated, great. Ammon is silenced, (v33). When God is in control, that's what happens. Joshua learnt at Ai, when he tried to do it his own way, that it's always God that wins the battle. Job done, finished, victory parade needed. But the vow overshadows everything.

A foolish vow

Vows were very common and vows were binding. Numbers 30:2: 'When a man makes a vow . . . he . . . must do everything he said.' Deuteronomy 23:21-23, 'Do not be slow to pay it when you've made a vow.' Jephthah's vow is the same (11:35). 'When he saw her, he tore his clothes . . . "Oh! My daughter! You have made me miserable . . . because I have made a vow to the LORD that I cannot break."'

What was the vow that he'd made? Verse 31: 'whatever comes out of the door of my house to meet me when I return in triumph from the Ammonites will be the LORD's, and I will sacrifice it as a burnt offering.' The glory of being God's salvation person is very short-lived. It sounds as though he offers up his daughter as a human sacrifice, something that we find repugnant. Did Jephthah think that anything other than a human being would be the first out of his door when he returned? It would be natural for the family to welcome the victor home. So why make such a vow?

It was his only child. The Bible's very clear about that. He only had one child; his precious daughter. What was he hoping for? Why say what he said? He was incredibly unwise to make such a vow because the consequences were so dire. The likelihood was that one of his own family would have to be sacrificed, because if you made a vow you had to stick with it.

Some people have argued other than the obvious – 'he did . . . as he . . . vowed' (v39). They have said that that means he committed his daughter to a lifelong holy sanctuary; he put her away as a thank offering for the great victory that he's achieved. That's why she had two months with her friends and after that she returned, he did as he vowed and put her away. Some say a God-fearing man like Jephthah couldn't have done this kind of thing. But the more I've read and studied it, I can't come to any other conclusion than that he had to do exactly as he said he would do in verse 31. And to be a burnt offering to me sounds final.

So he had to do it. It has to be said there is no other mention of human sacrifice in the whole of the Old Testament. I think the only conclusion that you can draw from this is that the man got out of control. Didn't Jesus say, 'Let your "Yes" be "Yes" and your "No" be "No"'? Be careful what you say. Don't promise something you cannot deliver. Do not overstate the case. Do not exaggerate. Let your speech be moderate. In those days, lots of people made vows of this sort. 'Oh if I get this, I will do this!' They would make extravagant claims and promises. If Jepthah had stopped and thought for one minute, surely he would never have said it. He makes this rash promise which he had to keep. She was sacrificed and she died.

I work in Christian committees, and I hear people make expansive promises and they never keep them. We need to be careful with our tongues. 'Let your "Yes" be "Yes" and your "No" be "No."' Don't make promises you can't keep.

Jephthah and Ephraim

The Ephraimites turn up. 'What do you mean by fighting Ammon without asking us?' they said. 'We're the boys. We like a battle.' And they turn up with an army (Judg. 12:1). This disagreement descends into racial abuse (v4): 'You Gileadites are renegades from Ephraim and Manasseh.' That's racial abuse. 'You're just the rump of two other tribes.'

Tragedy overshadows what should have been this wonderful moment. The thing I want to leave you with is this. It's only six years that Jephthah rules. And he's gone. Read the rest of the book of the Judges and you see things go from bad to worse. Salvation under that regime is only for a season. I think Judges is written for that reason. The rags to riches story would have been wonderful but it didn't work out. David, the best king that Israel ever had, ends up fancying another bloke's wife. So he bungs the husband in the front of the battle. Always, when God raises up the saviour in the Old Testament, it doesn't quite work: it's temporary. And the cry goes up, 'Where is the one who will save his people from their sins?' Nobody in the Old Testament lasts. They're all shown to be fallible, frail, human beings.

Judges is pointing us forward to the day when the Lord Jesus will come to save us from our sin. He will do it historically, verifiably, in a place where every man can see it. It's Jesus Christ, sat at the right hand of God, having been crucified, raised from the dead, the first-fruits, so that one day we will be with him because, as Jesus says, 'I am the way. I am the way this is going to happen.' That's the way the Old Testament paints salvation history: guys who do something good but often blow it afterwards. It points us to the one who never gets it wrong, who has saved us.

Do you know where else Jephthah's mentioned? He's in the hall of fame in Hebrews 11. It says 'who through faith conquered kingdoms, administered justice, and gained what was promised.' He was God's servant for a season – God's saviour.

Endnote

[1] Dale Ralph Davis, *Judges* (Nairn: Christian Focus, 2006).

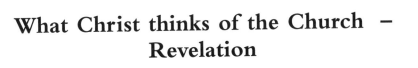

What Christ thinks of the Church –
Revelation

The cost of discipleship

by Jonathan Lamb

Jonathan Lamb

Jonathan is presently Director of Langham Preaching for Langham Partnership International, a global programme seeking to encourage a new generation of preachers and teachers. This is a ministry that networks with national leaders in many parts of the world, including Africa, Asia and Latin America as well as Central Europe and Eurasia.

Formerly a Chairman of Keswick Ministries and of Word Alive, Jonathan still serves as a Trustee for Keswick and regularly speaks at 'Keswicks' in other countries. Apart from teaching in a variety of contexts around the world, he is also a member of the preaching team at his local church, St Andrew's, in Oxford. He is married to Margaret and they have three daughters.

The cost of discipleship

Revelation 2:8-11

Introduction

A short while ago I met a Latvian pastor by the name of Josef Bondarenko. I wanted to speak with him because, over thirty years ago, I had his photograph on the wall in my student bed-sit. He had been a pastor in what was then the Soviet Union, and was one of many people who had been imprisoned for his faith. His photo – along with about thirty others – was placed on my wall as a daily reminder to pray for the church under pressure. He suffered three periods of imprisonment for proclaiming the Christian message, and many years in exile in Siberian work camps. And in his lecture to us some years after the collapse of the Soviet empire, he spoke movingly of the fact that his family still suffered the results of that period of hardship and exile, but shared his resolve to persevere in their Christian calling.

Of course, this is one example of what continues to happen the world over. It has been estimated that in 1999, 164,000 Christians died for their faith. At present it is estimated that some two hundred million evangelicals in 35 countries are suffering direct and hostile persecution. It's a reminder that the kind of pressure Josef Bondarenko faced is still exerted on thousands of Christians today. And though here in the West we might be tempted to lose sight of this, it is something we should expect. For the Christian life means being identified with Jesus Christ. If we follow in his steps as disciples, there is no question that it will be costly. As the apostles said in Acts 14:22, 'We must go through many hardships to enter the kingdom of God.' It's a condition of our discipleship.

The small church in Smyrna about whom John wrote understood this all too well, and we will learn much from the letter to the church which we find in Revelation 2. Revelation was written when the Roman empire extended across a huge territory, and it included present day Turkey. Smyrna is now called Izmir, the second city of Turkey. Writers often mention that it had an excellent harbour, flourishing trade, and a beautiful city overtopped by a hill with fine public buildings along the summit – referred to by one second century writer as the crown of Smyrna. It had been destroyed in 600BC, but later it rose from the ashes when Alexander the Great refounded the city. Another significant moment was when, in AD26, Smyrna successfully competed against eleven other cities to be the host city for a new temple built to deify the Emperor Tiberias, and it became the centre of the Caesar cult.

It is a very moving and tender letter, and it is unique in the collection of seven. The structure of the letters is usually shaped by a commendation, then a complaint, a command and then a promise to those who overcome. But the letter to the church in Smyrna is a beautiful letter of pastoral encouragement. And I hope it will be for us too. To be a Christian in Smyrna was to experience what it meant to be identified with Jesus and his cross. But they were also united with Jesus Christ in his life, and so we will look at both the costs and the certainties of Christian discipleship.

1. The costs of Christian discipleship

'I know your afflictions' (v9). The word 'afflictions' is the word frequently used in the New Testament for pressures. Paul used it a good deal in 2 Corinthians as he described the weight of suffering he endured, the crushing burdens he had to endure. It's a word which implies squeezing, grinding, threshing, beating – pressures of all kinds. What did that look like for the church in Smyrna?

The pressure of poverty

'I know your afflictions and your poverty' (v9). The word used for poverty implies destitution. They had absolutely nothing. The Christians were a despised minority in the city, and probably would have had a difficult time securing employment. We know that the Jewish population in the city hated the Christians, and could well have discriminated against them in commercial life. And we know from Hebrews what many early Christians had to face: 'Sometimes you were publicly exposed to insult and persecution . . . you joyfully accepted the confiscation of your property, because you knew that you yourselves had better and lasting possessions' (Heb. 10:33–34). The writer is saying the same as the risen Christ to Smyrna. You have better, more lasting possessions. You are suffering the pressure of poverty, Christ says, but spiritually you are rich.

It is surely significant that those parts of the world where the church is growing rapidly are mostly poor. On my travels I often meet pastors who can hardly afford a Bible, and who, without the money for a bicycle, walk miles to care for their congregations and the needy people all around them. But they are rich in faith, generous in their compassion, joyful in their daily ministry.

The pressure of slander

'I know the slander of those who say they are Jews and are not, but are a synagogue of Satan' (v9).

Jesus knew about another cost of discipleship, and this was the pressure exerted on them by the substantial Jewish population in the city. Much of the hatred towards Christians arose from the fact that it was from Jewish synagogues that the church drew so many of its converts. So the Christian community was the target for malicious gossip, including slanderous accusations of being disloyal to Rome. In fact, the words of Jesus here are very strong indeed: they are 'a synagogue of Satan'. They're not Jews at all, Jesus says; they don't deserve to be seen as the people of God, because they are doing the Devil's work. They are slandering – literally 'blaspheming' – the Christian community, and therefore blaspheming God himself.

Twice in this short letter the risen Christ refers to Satan's work – here in verse 9 and then again in verse 10, where he is referred to as the Devil, which means the accuser or the slanderer, the 'father of lies' as Jesus called him (Jn. 8:44). We can easily forget that there is a Devil actively working against us, and that Christian discipleship is lived out in the context of a spiritual battle. The Devil uses any means he can, including using so-called religious people as he did here in Smyrna. Here was another aspect of the cost of discipleship. Gossip, rumour, insult, abuse – they can be deeply painful, and in Smyrna they led to still worse pressure.

The pressure of persecution

'Do not be afraid of what you are about to suffer. I tell you, the devil will put some of you in prison to test you, and you will suffer persecution for ten days. Be faithful even to the point of death . . .' (v10).

Persecution, imprisonment and death were all predicted for this small faithful Christian community. The use of the words 'ten days' has generated a variety of comments. Some suggest it was a reference to the length of time of the athletic games and gladiatorial contests, found on some inscriptions in Smyrna: the 'ten-day games', in which Christians would be paraded as fodder for wild animals or helpless victims for the gladiators' sport. Others suggest it simply refers to a specific short period of time, much as we use the term 'a couple of weeks' or 'a fortnight.' In other words, it will be intense, but it will come to an end. But we hardly need to debate the point, for history tells us that imprisonment in those days was not like imprisonment today. When you walked from prison, you usually walked to your execution.

We know too that Smyrna was one of the cities where the Christian community faced the challenges associated with the Roman insistence on patriotic loyalty to the Emperor, especially because Smyrna was now the centre of the Caesar cult, with its fine temple erected to the honour of Tiberias. The faithful Christians rejected the call to sprinkle incense on the fire which burned before the effigy of Caesar, refusing to acknowledge him as Lord. And so they were accused of disloyalty and treachery.

The most well known Christian in Smyrna was one of John's own disciples, a man called Polycarp, who in the middle of the second century had to confront what Jesus predicted in verse 10: 'Be faithful, even to the point of death.' He was probably in the small church when the letter from John arrived, and many years later he became its pastoral leader. In AD156 he was hunted down and escorted to the hill above the city. There, surrounded by the fine public buildings – the 'crown' of Smyrna – he faced death. This is one early account of that day

> The proconsul urged him and said, 'Swear and I will release you. Curse the Christ.' Polycarp said, 'Eighty and six years have I served him and he has done me no wrong. How then can I blaspheme my king who saved me?' Then said the proconsul, 'I have wild beasts. If you do not repent, I will throw you to them.' But he said, 'Send for them. For repentance from better to worse is not a change permitted to us.' Then said the proconsul again, 'If you despise the wild beasts, I will have you to be consumed by fire, if you do not repent.' And Polycarp answered, 'You threaten the fire that burns for an hour and in a little while is quenched. For you do not know the fire of the judgement to come, and the fire of the eternal punishment reserved for the ungodly. But why do you delay? Do what you will.'

And on the hill that day he was burnt alive, knowing what the risen Jesus had written to him and that small believing community sixty years earlier: 'Be faithful, even to the point of death, and I will give you the crown of life.' It was not the glory of the city, but the crown that endures.

The pressure of poverty, of slander, of persecution; these were some of the costs of discipleship. For the sake of Christ they lost their material goods, their reputation, their freedom, even life itself. Why did they do it? All around the world the same is happening, and why do they do it? Because it is true. Because the Christian life means we are united to Jesus Christ, and Jesus Christ promised that 'in the world you will have tribulation.' These are the costs of Christian discipleship.

2. The certainties of Christian discipleship

For the church in Smyrna there were very significant reminders of the certainties associated with their identification with Jesus. If their suffering was because they were united with Jesus in his death, what would it mean for them to be united to Christ in his glorious resurrection?

The certainty of Christ's presence

We have seen in verse 9 how Jesus begins his tender letter – 'I know the pressure you are under, I know your afflictions.' How was that possible? In John's vision in Revelation 1 we are told that Jesus walks among the lampstands – among the churches. He is with his people. I wonder if, when you are going through a tough time, you know something of the comfort of a good friend with whom you can share the burden. It can make a huge difference. And for me there is enormous comfort in those introductory words: 'I know.' When I was a child, we had an old 78 record with Paul Robeson singing some of the songs of the plantation slaves: 'Nobody knows the trouble I've seen. Nobody knows but Jesus.'

Let me marshall just a few witnesses. Paul, at the end of his life, in Roman dungeon, cold, lonely, deserted and close to martyrdom: 'But the Lord stood at my side and gave me strength.' Sheila Cassidy tells the story of a Bible found in a detention centre in Chile. An unknown Christian, the victim of the secret police, had written inside: 'I could only close my eyes and hold his hand and grit my teeth and know with cold, dark, naked knowing that God was there.' Betsie Ten Boom in the Ravensbruck concentration camp: 'We must tell people that there is no pit so deep that he is not deeper still.' Or Richard Baxter: 'Christ leads me through no darker rooms than he went through before.' We need this word of encouragement, for many of us confront demanding pressures or carry some debilitating burden. The costs of discipleship are very real indeed. Please don't miss this comforting certainty – the certainty of Christ's presence. And what gives such pressure meaning is our vital connection with Jesus. We suffer in solidarity with Jesus who took our sufferings upon himself.

We have been glad to have had friendship with the Roseveare family in the past, and to have met Dr Helen Roseveare, who served as a medical missionary in what was then Zaire. During the revolutions of the 1960s she faced beatings and torture and rape. She tells in her writing of an occasion when, as she was close to being executed, the Holy Spirit reminded her of her calling: 'Twenty years ago you asked me for the privilege of being a missionary, the privilege of being identified with me. This is it. Don't you want it? This is what it means. These are not your sufferings; they are my sufferings. All I ask of you is the loan of your body.' She was spared execution and later wrote: 'He didn't stop the sufferings. He didn't stop the wickedness, the cruelties, the humiliation or anything. It was all there. The pain was just as bad. The fear was just as bad. But it was altogether different. It was in Jesus, for Him, with Him.'

The great certainty for Polycarp, for the hard-pressed Christians in Smyrna, and for you and me, is that – no matter what happens – the suffering and risen Christ is with us.

The certainty of God's control

We have seen in the text the two references to Satan's work. In verse 9 we noted the actions of those inspired by Satan himself; and in verse 10 it is the Devil who would put some of them in prison. It is worth a few minutes reflecting on this issue. It is sadly true that talk of principalities and powers, of Satan and evil spirits, surprises and even amuses some Christians. As far as they are concerned, it is all some superstitious anachronism that belongs to an outdated worldview. But many Christians are all too aware of the reality of evil and dark forces.

I was recently at a conference when an accident happened to one of the children of a fellow speaker. His son was climbing a tree shortly before the evening event at which his father was due to speak. Unfortunately he fell, his arm was in severe pain, an ambulance was called, and he was whisked away to hospital. After the evening   meeting, several of us discussed the incident over coffee. What lay behind it, what was its cause? On the one hand, it happened before his father was to give a major address, so it must have been Satanic intrusion: it was spiritual warfare. On the other hand, you could answer by saying that it was the result a combination of a typically active ten year old and the force of gravity.

There are many times in our lives when we ask such questions. Why does God allow this? Why am I under such sustained attack? Some Christians appear to live their lives as if they are in a Star Wars adventure – they are surrounded by equal and opposite forces of good and evil. Neither good nor evil is quite strong enough, and so we assign this part of our life or this event exclusively to God, and another part to the Devil. It's almost as if there are two worlds of good and evil, with our own lives swinging between the two. This isn't the biblical perspective, but it is a surprisingly common feature of supposed Christian spirituality.

Then we might also meet some Christians with a different perspective. In their view, God is good, and whenever something enters their life which is clearly evil, God *must* remove it in response to our prayer of faith. And if the evil doesn't disappear, it is because our faith is insufficiently strong. And neither is this the true biblical perspective.

It's clear from the New Testament that Christians experienced Satanic resistance. But the context of Jesus' words to the church in Smyrna show us that this was not out of control. It is worth noticing in verse 10 that only some of them were put in prison, and the persecution was for a defined period. There were limits imposed. As in the story of Job, the situation was still under the Lord's oversight and care. We can affirm that nothing lies outside the scope of God's sovereignty and control, not even Satan. He can only act within the parameters which God has set. Even the worst of Satan's activities may be redeemed by God to fulfil his own purposes, and we are to live as faithful children of the Sovereign God. His purpose is not to by-pass difficulties in our lives, but to transform them. And this is linked to the most obvious certainty of this letter.

The certainty of death's defeat

In each of the letters the designation given to Christ at the beginning of the letter is often specially appropriate to the particular situation of that church. Many of the phrases used to introduce Christ are borrowed from the earlier vision in Revelation 1. This is one of the integrating features of the three chapters, and why we are meant to read the letters together. They give us a composite view of the diverse challenges and opportunities of the churches, and a composite view of Jesus himself. To Smryna: 'These are the words of him who is the First and the Last, who died and came to life again' (v8).

This phrase 'the First and the Last' was used of God himself in Isaiah 44:6. And John has used it in chapter 1:8,17 and also at the end of Revelation. Jesus, God's Son, is at the beginning and at the end. He is Lord of life. Here in verse 8 the tense of the verb refers to the act, the moment of resurrection. 'He became dead and lived again.' The Christians in Smyrna would have listened attentively. They lived in a city which had been destroyed and then rebuilt, which had died and been resurrected. And death hung over them. So the words of the One who had defeated death represented another certainty in their Christian discipleship. C.S. Lewis once commented that Jesus had forced open a door locked since Adam's death; and in doing so he had beaten death itself, bringing mankind into an entirely new existence.

Our hope for the future is based on an event which has already happened. Usually our hopes are to do with something that has not yet occurred. We look at the possibilities and say, 'I hope it will be like this.' 'I hope it will be a sunny day tomorrow.' 'I hope the preacher will sit down soon.' But there are no guarantees! Christian hope is radically different. It *will* be realised. It is totally certain. Why? Because it is based on an event which has already happened. As Peter wrote, 'hope through the resurrection of Jesus Christ from the dead.' Jesus, who died and who sprang to life again; Jesus the first and the last, the Lord of life. You are united to him. He is the unchanging God. From the beginning of time to its end, he is the Sovereign Lord.

The certainty of Christ's presence; the certainty of God's control; the certainty of death's defeat. And finally,

The certainty of eternal reward

'Be faithful, even to the point of death, and I will give you the crown of life. He who has an ear, let him hear what the Spirit says to the churches. He who overcomes will not be hurt at all by the second death' (vs10–11).

The promised reward is a crown of life. This is possibly the image of the crown of victory in the games, or a laurel crown as a reward for service in the city. Perhaps there is an echo of the 'crown of the city' high on the hill. But probably it refers to the royal crown, the reward to faithful disciples who will rule with Christ. And not only that, verse 11 assures us that the faithful disciple 'will not be hurt at all by the second death.' This is the phrase used by John later in the book, which helps us understand its meaning: 'Then death and Hades are thrown into the lake of fire. The lake of fire is the second death' (Rev. 20:14). The second death is the death of eternal judgement. It is the death after death. We all die once, but the second death is an eternity separated from God. And for Christ's followers this death will not touch us. It is an emphatic double negative in verse 11. There is no way you will ultimately be harmed. You are absolutely secure.

These then are the costs and the certainties of discipleship, the suffering and the glory. They belong together. 'We must go through many hardships to enter the kingdom of God.' These many pressures are a gateway, for that is how we enter the kingdom of God. Troubles are not a dead end, but the way out to life in all its fullness. So my brothers and sisters, let us hear what the Spirit says. 'Do not be afraid . . . Be faithful.' 'If we endure, we will also reign with him.'

Why holiness matters

by Tim Chester

Tim Chester

Tim Chester is part of the Crowded House, a church-planting initiative in Sheffield. He is director of the Northern Training Institute and was previously Research and Policy Director for Tearfund. He is the author of a number of books, including *The Message of Prayer, Good News to the Poor, Delighting in the Trinity* and *The Busy Christian's Guide to Busyness*. He is series editor of the Good Book Guides and co-author of an evangelistic Bible overview, called *The World We All Want*. He is married with two daughters

Why holiness matters

Revelation 2:18–29

Introduction

There is an annual 'Take your daughter to work' day. The aim is to break down some of the prejudices about women's roles. Since the church that I lead meets in a home, I'm not sure what it would mean to take them to work with me. In fact, in my home, it's the women who go to work and I'm left behind to do some laundry.

How would you feel if a member of your family came to work with you? Think back to the last day you spent at work or a day you spent at home. Imagine a family member with you all the time. What would they make of your conduct? What would your church make of it? Would the person they see be the person they see every Sunday morning? The letter to Thyatira is all about what happens when Sunday and Monday don't match.

What about a 'Take your God to work' day? How would that feel? Look at verses 18-19. 'To the angel of the church in Thyatira write: These are the words of the Son of God, whose eyes are like blazing fire and whose feet are like burnished bronze. I know your deeds, your love and faith, your service and perseverance, and that you are now doing more than you did at first.'

The Son of God's eyes are like blazing fire and he knows our deeds. He is watching us on Monday mornings. And in Thyatira what Jesus sees is their love, faith, service and perseverance, and he commends them for it. He commends them for their progress. Here was a church that was making progress, growing in love, faith and service. They could look back and see how they had progressed. And yet the words of Christ are 'I have this against you.' There is still a battle for holiness to be fought.

The battle for an undivided life

Verse 20: 'Nevertheless, I have this against you: You tolerate that woman Jezebel, who calls herself a prophetess. By her teaching she misleads my servants into sexual immorality and the eating of food sacrificed to idols.' Does it strike you as odd that this church, growing in love, faith and service, should tolerate immorality? It is a bit more subtle and a bit closer to home.

Come with me to Thyatira. Thyatira was a commercial hub in Asia Minor. Lydia, the first convert in Philippi, was a dealer in purple cloth from the city of Thyatira. She is on a business trip there when she gets converted. It is a place with many trade guilds: trade guilds for potters, bakers, wool merchants, slave traders, coppersmith, clothiers, tanners and shoe-makers. These were central to the commercial life of the city. If you wanted to progress, you needed to network in these trade guilds, but these involved pagan rituals and sacrifices. Verse 20 talks about eating foods sacrificed to idols. Imagine meeting together with your trade guild. There the sacrifice was made, the food handed round. Not only that, but they were steeped in the cult of the Roman Emperor. Worshipping Caesar as God began in Asia Minor among the churches that John is writing to. They were the beneficiaries of Roman rule, and so they pledged allegiance to Caesar; they praised him for bringing peace and prosperity to the world.

To be part of a trade guild, you needed to offer food to idols, to worship the emperor. So what do you do? It seems that Jezebel was saying 'Sacrifice food to idols, pledge allegiance to Caesar. It's not a big deal: what choice do you have? On Sunday pledge Jesus as Lord and on Monday pledge Caesar as Lord.'

When the risen Christ talks here about immorality, he may be talking about literal immoral acts that were involved in some pagan rituals, but probably there is more to it than that. If you turn to Revelation 17, in the opening verses we read that one of the seven angels who had the seven bowls said, 'Come, I will show you the punishment of the great prostitute, who sits on many waters. With her the kings of the earth committed adultery and the inhabitants of the earth were intoxicated with the wine of her adulteries.' He's talking about Rome and the Roman system, and he says the kings of the world have committed adultery with her. You get a similar statement at the beginning of chapters 18 and 19. Immorality in the book of Revelation is a picture of compromise. It is spiritual adultery. That's why he calls this prophetess Jezebel.

Jezebel was the foreign queen who married Ahab and introduced the worship of Baal alongside the worship of the Lord. It wasn't that the Israelites ditched worshipping the Lord and worshipped Baal instead: they did the two side by side. In the same way, the Jezebel of Thyatira is not *outside* the church, she is *inside* the church, worshipping Jesus, but on Monday morning worshipping other gods.

Do you have two sets of values? On Sunday you believe God's word as it speak of Jesus Christ, on Monday you believe a thousand adverts that say that life and identity and fulfilment are found through what you can buy. On Sunday you entrust your future to the sovereign Lord, on Monday you entrust your future to HSBC. The battle for holiness is a battle for an undivided life.

I want you to sympathise with Jezebel for a moment. How will you get on with life? How will you prosper if you're not part of a trade guild? Many of you may deal with similar dilemmas. How will you get on with life, how will you prosper in the workplace, how will you get a husband or a wife unless you're prepared to compromise a bit? But Jesus calls her 'Jezebel.' She 'misleads' her servants, and that is only used in Revelation of Satan, his false prophet and Babylon the Prostitute (Rev. 12:9,13:14, 18:23, 20:3,8,10).

Does your conversation reflect the Lordship of Jesus over all your life? Or does your conversation mirror the concerns and priorities of the world? Think of those Christmas letters that you write. I find that the Christmas letters of Christians fall into two categories. There are those who are full of 'what we've been doing with the church, and oh, by the way we went on holiday.' Then there are Christmas letters that are like a travelling itinerary of 'all the wonderful places that we've visited, oh, by the way we're still part of the church.' Is yours an undivided life? Because the message of Christ is no compromise.

Look at verse 18 again: 'These are the words of the Son of God.' Caesar was called a son of God, or he was the called the son of Zeus. The Son of God challenges these claims head on. There can be no accommodation between Christ and Caesar, between Christ and the world.

The Jezebel option leads to judgement (vs 22,23): 'So I will cast her on a bed of suffering, and I will make those who commit adultery with her suffer intensely, unless they repent of her ways. I will strike her children dead.' In the Old Testament, Jezebel's children end up slaughtered. Whether it is literal or not here, the meaning is clear. Compromise leads to judgment.

The battle for an undivided heart

The risen Lord has eyes like blazing fire. What is he looking at? Verse 23: 'Then all the churches will know that I am he who searches hearts and minds, and I will repay each of you according to your deeds.' He is looking at our hearts.

It would be very easy to define worldliness in terms of *activities* that Christians shouldn't do and *places* that Christians shouldn't go. But the battleground for holiness is our own hearts. Oliver Cromwell wrote this to his niece: 'Anything that steals the heart's affections from Christ: that is the world.' There are Christians leading respectable lives with exemplary behaviour who are losing the battle for the heart. Their actions arise from duty instead of grace, and they produce self-righteousness instead of glory for God. Verse 23 is a quote from Jeremiah 17, 'The heart is deceitful above all things and beyond all cure; who can understand it?' And the answer comes 'I the LORD search the heart and examine the mind, to reward a man according to his conduct, according to what his deeds deserve' (Jer. 17:9-10).

Why is the heart so important? Jeremiah has just told us

> This is what the LORD says. 'Cursed is the one who trust in man, who depends on flesh for his strength and whose heart turns away from the LORD. He will be like a bush in the wastelands; he will not see prosperity when it comes. He will dwell in the parched places of the desert, in a salt land where no one lives.
>
> But blessed is the man who trusts in the LORD, whose confidence is in him. He will be like a tree planted by the water that sends its roots by the stream. It does not fear when heat comes; its leaves are always green (Jer. 17:5-8).

'The heat will come', says the Lord through Jeremiah. Adversity, suffering, trials and problems will come to us all. What makes the difference is our hearts. If our hearts turn away from the Lord, when the heat comes we will be like a bush in the desert. But if we trust in the Lord, we will be like a tree planted by the water.

I remember two elderly women in a previous church. One of them suffered from pain in her legs, and whenever you met her, that was all she talked about. She moaned about the pain she was feeling. The other one, a very godly woman called Ruth, suffered for many years with crippling arthritis. In the later months of her life, she suffered from cancer, and yet when you spoke to her, her conversation was either full of asking what you were doing or full of the Lord. I remember her smile. She was full of joy. What made the difference between these two women were not circumstances but a heart that was trusting in the Lord.

I want to take you through the keyhole to my study. At 7:30am each morning you will see me reading my Bible, praying, calm, trusting, at peace with God and the world. Ladies and gentleman, I am a picture of godliness! But if you hang around for half an hour and you see me go downstairs to usher my daughters to school. Invariably they are not ready, they are arguing with each other and with me, and I get angry. My heart's desire, my idolatrous desire for an ordinary quiet life, has run smack into two girls who have their own ideas.

I lead a divided life. What I've come to realise is that it's the me at 8am who is the real me. I desire the kingdom of God, but I also desire the kingdom of Tim. Jesus says that from within, out of men's hearts, come 'evil thoughts, sexual immorality, theft, adultery, greed, malice, deceit, lewdness, envy, slander, arrogance and folly. All these evils come from inside and make a man "unclean"' (Mk. 7:21-23). These flow out of our hearts: the desire for control or possessions or respect or affirmation or approval, often good desires but desires that have grown bigger to us than God himself.

Psalm 86:11 says 'Teach me your way, O LORD, and I will walk in your truth; give me an undivided heart, that I may fear your name.' Elsewhere the psalmist speaks of a fixed heart, a heart that is steadfast. We live in a world of such variety. We live in a time when people change their sets of values in different contexts. The challenge for us is to have a heart that is fixed on serving Jesus.

Notice that we are in it together. Holiness is a community project. This is how the writer to the Hebrews puts it: 'See to it, brothers, that none of you has a sinful, unbelieving heart that turns away from the living God. But encourage one another daily, as long as it is called Today so that none of you may be hardened by sin's deceitfulness.'

Let me tell you one of my favourite Bible stories. It's the story of Elijah on Mount Carmel. Elijah there confronts the Israelites because they are worshipping the Lord and worshipping Baal. His challenge to them is 'How long will you waver among two opinions? If the LORD is God, follow him; but if Baal is God, follow him' (1 Kgs. 18:21). And so he sets up this challenge and the prophets of Baal build up this altar and prepare the sacrifice and call upon Baal to light the sacrifice. We read 'there was no response, no one answered; no one paid attention.'

Then it's Elijah's turn. He builds an altar, prepares a sacrifice and puts lots of water on, which wasn't required: he's just making God's job harder for him. He steps forward and prays to God and 'Oomph!' this fire starts, which not only lights the sacrifice but consumes the whole altar. And the people worship God.

Can you remember who Elijah's great opponent was in this? Jezebel. The prophets of Baal are eating at her table. She has been executing the prophets of God. So when God calls the prophetess Jezebel in Thyatira he's evoking this story. He's reminding us of the Carmel challenge: 'How long will you waver among two opinions?'

I love to imagine myself as Elijah, being a real hero for God, bold and content in my faith. The reality is that I'm much more like one of the wavering Israelites. The Carmel challenge is being re-enacted in our hearts every day. Not many of us face these big set pieces like Elijah does. For us, the battle for holiness is fought in a thousand small moments, but each time it is the Carmel challenge, and it calls for us to be bold like Elijah.

The battle to hold on to the gospel

Look again at this word to Thyatira: 'Only hold on to what you have until I come' (v25). The only command is to hold on. The risen Christ commends them for not following 'deep things.' Look at verse 24: 'Now I say to the rest of you in Thyatira, to you who do not hold to her teaching and have not learnt Satan's so-called deep secrets . . .' That might be ironic, it may be that Jezebel talked about the deep secrets of God and the risen Christ says really it's the deep secrets of Satan. Or it maybe that Jezebel's followers claimed to follow the ways of Satan so that they could take part in these pagan rituals without being affected.

Either way, the point is that Jesus rejects so-called deep things. We already have the wisdom and the power of God in the message of Christ crucified. There is no higher way, no special teaching, no advanced message. The secret of holiness is no secret at all; it is to hold on to the gospel, the goodness, grace and sovereignty of God.

That doesn't mean it's easy. It's still a battle. Behind every sin is a lie, a false promise. The battle for holiness is a battle to believe the truth. The truth is that only God can bring true joy. It's a lie that we need to prove ourselves. The truth is that God justifies us through grace. John Piper says that the 'fight of faith is the fight to keep your heart contented in Christ, to really believe and keep on believing that he will meet every need and satisfy every longing.'[1]

I don't want you to think of the battle for holiness as a kind of dreary battle where you have to give up pleasure because you must. It is the battle to delight in God. C.S. Lewis famously said that our problem is not that we have desires that we have to satisfy, but that we are too easily satisfied.

The battle to hold on to the heavenly perspective

In a sense the battle for holiness is a battle for our imaginations. That's why the book of Revelation is so full of rich imagery; it's pointing us to the perspective of heaven. What we see is the world around us, a world where wicked people prosper, which tells us that shopping or sex are the mark of a good life, in which market forces and global corporations seem supreme, and all the time we are invited to sign up.

In the book of Revelation things are always being opened in heaven for us to see. John gives us a different perspective and take on reality. Look at verses 26–28: 'To him who overcomes and does my will to the end, I will give authority over the nations – "He will rule them with an iron sceptre; he will dash them to pieces like pottery" – just as I have received authority from the Father. I will also give him the morning star.'

Here is a vision of success; we can overcome, we can have authority. The morning star is the planet Venus, a Roman symbol of victory. The generals erected temples to the goddess Venus and carried her symbols on their standards. Success, authority, victory; but the risen Christ turns our ideas of success and victory upside down. Verse 27 is a quote from Psalm 2 and in that psalm God gives to his Son authority over the nations. Now Jesus says that he is giving that authority to his people, and that is what happened at the Great Commission. Jesus says to his disciples, 'All authority in heaven and on earth has been given to me. Therefore go and make disciples of all nations, baptising them in the name of the Father and the Son and the Holy Spirit, and teaching them to obey everything that I have commanded.' All authority has been given to Jesus, therefore he sends us out to the nations to teach them to obey the commands of Jesus. That's how we exercise authority through the nations, through his word.

The same words from Psalm 2 are quoted in Revelation 12 and there we are told what it means to overcome: 'They overcame him [Satan] by the blood of the lamb and the word of their testimony; they did not love their lives so much to shrink from death' (Rev.12:11). How do we overcome? How do we exercise authority? By the blood of the lamb. It's so topsy turvy; we rule by serving, we conquer by loving, we overcome by suffering. At the heart of this vision and at the very centre of heaven is a lamb looking as if it has been slaughtered. This is the empire of the lamb.

Look at verse 28: 'I will also give him the morning star.' At the end of Revelation Jesus says that he is the morning star. The morning star (the planet Venus) is seen in the sky just before dawn. Jesus says that he himself is the sign of a new day. He is assuring us that we will be a part of God's new dawn, God's new age. We will see God's kingdom, we will share God's banquet, and what we shall see on that day is Jesus.

So come back with me to Thyatira where the Christians have to choose between success in life and remaining faithful to God. It's the decision that we all make between worldliness and holiness, and as we face that choice, Jesus is raising our sights. Faithfulness might mean suffering and hardship in this life, but beyond that is the dawn of a world made new, in which God dwells with his people. The battle for holiness is battle for an undivided life and an undivided heart. It's the battle to hold on to the gospel and onto the heavenly perspective.

As we end, let me take you to another mountain. Here again is a contest, only this time it is Jesus challenging the powers of darkness. Here is a sacrifice, although this time it is the Son of God on the altar. Here again is the fire of God's judgement falling, only this time it falls on his Son in our place. Isaiah speaks prophetically of this judgment in that great chapter 53, 'He was pierced for our transgressions, he was crushed for our iniquities' and in chapter 55:1-2 he gives us the invitation that's God's invitation to us. These are words that I often speak to my own heart when struggling with temptation

Come, all you who are thirsty, come to the waters;
and you who have no money, come buy and eat!
Come, buy wine and milk without money and without cost.
Why spend money on what is not bread,
and your labour on what does not satisfy?
Listen, listen to me and eat what is good,
and your soul will delight in the richest fare.

How long will you waver between two opinions?

Endnotes

[1] John Piper, *Future Grace* (Multnomah/IVP, 1995), p222.

Reputation and Reality

by Jonathan Lamb

Revelation 3:1-6

Introduction

The Steven Spielberg movie, *Catch me if you can*, was based on the true story of an American conman who, before his nineteenth birthday, pocketed $2.5 million in the 1960s by forging cheques and taking on a variety of clever disguises. They included pretending to be a Pan Am pilot, a paediatrician, and a lawyer. The tag line of the film was: 'The true story of a real fake.' More recently, I read of a man who managed to sustain a profligate lifestyle based on credit card fraud by posing as a variety of people: as a golf partner of Bill Clinton, then the boss of a chain of Las Vegas casinos, and then inventor of part of the space shuttle. But we needn't look at the extreme examples, for we know the tendency all too well. Most of us indulge in a degree of play-acting for the cameras, of course. When in public our manners improve, our dress might be smarter, our annoying habits under control, even our accent slightly more proper. Most of us, at one time or another, pretend to be someone we are not.

Many politicians and priests are undermined by the public's perception of spin, corruption or a lack of integrity. And we know the

problem in our own lives too: maintaining an image, when underneath things are not what they should be. I recently read an interesting news item which described the arrest of a German businessman.
'Heinrich of Frankfurt has been given a ten month suspended
sentence and fined a thousand Euros for assaulting a traffic policeman.
"Here's something for your mouth," shouted Heinrich, as he punched
the policeman in the face after the policeman refused to remove the
ticket from his illegally parked vehicle. Heinrich is an anger management consultant.'

Yet most people, if they are honest, are hungry to discover what is
real. In a world of spin, we are looking for something genuine. In a
world of virtual experience, we want reality. In a world of image, we
want substance. And that is exactly what the risen Christ wants of his
church. His verdict on the church in Sardis is devastatingly brief.

1. Reputation and reality

'I know your deeds; you have a reputation of being alive, but you are
dead' (v1).

Unlike Jesus' assessment of the previous churches, he doesn't com-
mend them but only rebukes them. Certainly the church in Sardis has
'a name', a reputation. As far as most people were concerned, it was a
live and active congregation. It certainly would not be what most of
us might call a dead church. Sardis was the kind of church that would
have made it into the church growth books. It probably had a large
and a growing congregation. Its programme was full, its budget was
healthy, its web site was impressive. But in reality it was dead. Its supposed image of life and vitality was little more than a façade, and Jesus
saw behind the mask; he looked beneath the surface. And his verdict
continues in verse 2: 'I have not found your deeds complete in the
sight of my God.' Your deeds are incomplete; they are not fulfilled,
they haven't met God's standards, his purpose for you as a Christian
community. The church in Sardis should have displayed more of the
qualities we looked at in Thyatira, described in Revelation 2:19: 'I
know your deeds, your love, your faith, your service and perseverance.'

And Christ says to them that their deeds are not complete 'in the sight of God'. It's an intriguing phrase. The idea appears frequently in Paul's writing in 2 Corinthians. Paul carried out his work under God's watching eye. He frequently referred to God as his witness. He was aware of the fact that what really mattered was not the impressive rhetoric or glossy image of the so-called super-apostles in Corinth, not the superficial bluster but the authentic, genuine service, carried out with God watching.

And this is the distinction made in verse 2. We can impress onlookers, we can polish up our image, but there is a difference between what the outside observer sees and what God sees. Primarily, we are accountable to God. As the Lord said to Samuel when looking for the king: 'Man looks at the outward appearance, but the Lord looks at the heart' (1 Sam. 16:7). He can see how much reality there is behind the profession, how much genuine spiritual life there is behind our carefully groomed image.

The church at Sardis didn't seem to attract the opposition of the Jews, or the persecution of the Romans; it didn't appear to have the internal threats of heresy. It was quite comfortable. During its history, the city of Sardis felt itself secure. It was built 450 metres above the Hermus valley, an acropolis that was like a giant watchtower, surrounded on three sides by cliffs. The residents were tempted to feel that the city was impregnable. And like the city itself, the church suffered from the same complacency. They felt themselves to be secure. They weren't aware of any problem at all, which is why Jesus had to call it to wake up, as we'll see.

There is a clue to its inconsistency in verse 4. It might have had the right image, but it had compromised with the culture of the city. Christ indicates that there were at least a few believers who were not part of the general spiritual stagnation, who are described as 'people who have not soiled their clothes.' Sardis had a reputation for bad character, and in a subtle way the church had become contaminated. Underneath the respectable exterior, the image of orthodoxy, there was corruption.

We know that what Jesus is describing is all too often true of churches but also of our own lives. I sometimes feel this acutely, aware on the one hand of what I long to be as a follower of Jesus Christ, yet also aware of the pull in the other direction, and the temptation to pretend to be someone different. For churches this can happen in a range of ways.

Nominalism: this is one of the greatest problems within our own continent. Sometimes called 'notionalism', this describes the situation where upwards of 95 per cent might tick the box 'Christian', but where there is no real faith, no committed Christian discipleship. We describe it as nominal – Christian in name only. Apparently 72 per cent of Britain's population consider themselves Christian. But 48 per cent do not understand that Easter marks the death and resurrection of Jesus. I'm not sure things are much better in the US: barely one in three knows that the Sermon on the Mount was preached by Jesus (and 12 per cent apparently think that Joan of Arc was the wife of Noah!) But nominalism is a danger for us all, and the Bible has a great deal to say about outward appearance and inward reality. It is very easy for us to fall into the trap which the Lord spoke about through Isaiah: 'These people come near to me with their mouth, and honour me with their lips, but their hearts are far from me.'

Activism: this is one of the temptations of our churches and of some Christians too. We can fill our diaries, we can run our churches as if Jesus had said, 'I am come that you might have meetings, meetings in abundance.' But again we must not confuse activity with life. Sometimes our activism can be a façade for an empty spiritual life. Sometimes it can even create that emptiness.

Formalism: a church is in danger of death when it becomes more concerned with structures and forms than with spiritual life. Peter Drucker, the management guru, once observed that, after a certain period of time, organisations tend to settle down to doing things right rather than doing the right things. They are keen to keep the machinery running smoothly, but fail to ensure that their primary strategic objectives are maintained. And it can be the same for churches: we can do things right, but it can ultimately be spiritually empty.

Pharisaism: Jesus had a good deal to say about the religious people of his day, who gave alms, said their prayers, and tried to gain a reputation of being religious. 'Woe to you, the teachers of the law and Pharisees, you hypocrites! You are like white-washed tombs, which look beautiful on the outside but on the inside are full of dead men's bones, and everything unclean. In the same way, on the outside you appear to people as righteous but on the inside you are full of hypocrisy and wickedness.' The word hypocrisy comes from the word for an actor, someone who plays a part. It is the word for the religious fake. It is a world of make-believe. And in church life it can lead us, like Sardis, to imagine all is well and to judge church life by externals. Comparisons between churches can often be measured by numbers, by the standard of performance, or by income. Christian leaders can be measured by career path, speaking skills, influence in the evangelical world, or the size of their church.

In all of these ways, then, we can have reputation without reality. Personally or corporately, we can have the reputation of being alive, when in fact we are close to spiritual death.

2. Remember and repent

In verses 2 and 3 there is a cluster of words of exhortation, and we sense the urgency of Christ as he calls the church to respond. And it is heartening to see them, because it implies it is not too late to take action.

Wake up and strengthen

The underlying weakness at Sardis was that she assumed she was strong and secure. She hadn't realised how true spiritual life was being eroded. Sardis had defences which seemed impregnable. Many writers tell the story of Cyrus who once attacked the city. He wanted to capture it quickly so that he could sustain his military advance, and so he announced to his troops a special reward for anyone who could work out how to scale the cliffs and take the fortress.

One soldier studied it carefully and saw that there were relatively few guards and they hardly took their job seriously. And as a group of these guards reached over the walls to look at something on the cliff face, one of them leant too far and his helmet fell off. So he climbed over the wall, went down the path of a mountain goat, and retrieved his helmet. That night the watching soldier led a party up the cliff and into the city. What appeared to be so secure was taken relatively easily. And the same happened two hundred years later with a subsequent siege.

The Lord says the church is such a city: Watch! Wake up! Jesus said this several times in his public ministry: Watch and pray. Be dressed, and ready, with your lamps burning. And verse 2 continues: 'Strengthen what remains and is about to die.' Their spiritual life was almost non-existent, and the embers needed to be fanned into flame. The word strengthen is often used for the nurture of Christians. Such strengthening and nurturing is a vital part of church life and growth. It is needed for young Christians who are facing many new challenges; and it is needed by older Christians who are in danger of becoming spiritually stagnant.

Christianity Today published a report a while ago which suggested that, at least in some parts of the western world, there was emerging a consumerist attitude in the church. It was described as a 'McChurch mentality'. It suggested that congregations approached sermons in much the same way as they approached fast food restaurants. Today, McDonald's; tomorrow, Burger King. Paul did not set out to make passive listeners or spectators. He longed for changed lives, for committed disciples. So in Acts you'll notice they engaged in 'strengthening and encouraging' the disciples to remain true to the faith. But the exhortation was not just 'wake up and strengthen.'

Remember and repent

'Remember, therefore, what you have received and heard; obey it and repent' (v3).

What had they received? On the one hand the language implies that they had received the gospel, the word of the Lord which they had heard. They needed not just to remember that, but to see their lives shaped by that gospel truth. But they had also received the Holy Spirit. It would have remained a dead church if they had not realised their need of the Spirit's presence and empowering. The introduction to the letter refers to Christ with a distinct emphasis. 'These are the words of him who holds the seven spirits of God and the seven stars' (v1).

The 'seven spirits' is John's usual way of describing the Holy Spirit, and it is descriptive of the many ministries of the Spirit, the complete work of God in the Spirit's ministry of regeneration and renewal. Only the life-giving Spirit can fan the embers, restore us to spiritual life and vitality. And the 'seven stars' are the churches themselves, held in Christ's hand. Despite all we have said, this frail and feeble community is being held by the Lord. That is our only hope.

'Remember what you have received and heard': the word and the Spirit are the two essentials for spiritual life and vitality. It is fundamental to evangelical life that we retain this balance, and that we give our energies to receive what the Spirit says through God's word. Religious fakes only mark their Bibles. True disciples allow the Bible to mark them.

And perhaps it is worth a moment to comment on the phrase which appears in each of the seven letters, and is here in verse 6, because it relates to the significance of remembering God's word. 'He who has an ear, let him hear what the Spirit says to the churches.' In our work in Langham Partnership we are indebted to John Stott, not least for his clear insistence on the authority of Scripture. And he comments on this verse in a way which is helpful to us. Verse 6 conveys three vital truths about listening to what God is saying in Scripture.

First, although it was written by John, through his words the Holy Spirit is speaking. We often call this the double-authorship of Scripture. There are multiple human authors, but it is the word of God himself.

Second, each letter is written to a particular church, yet the Spirit is speaking to 'all of the churches.' So there is a universal application of Scripture, even if it is written in the first instance to particular people in particular historical contexts. It is a living word of God which the Spirit speaks to the churches.

Third, each letter was written many months before it was finally read by the recipients, as the postman trudged his way several hundred miles from city to city in western Turkey. But through these letters we are to hear what the Spirit 'is saying' continuously. It is not a dead letter, but a living voice.

These three basic convictions about the Bible are very significant. Whilst written centuries ago by various authors to a particular readership, the Spirit is speaking with a living voice to the whole church in every age and culture. And this is an essential element in the call of the risen Christ here in verse 3 to 'remember what you received and heard.' The only way to be revived, to be made alive, to be strengthened in the faith, is through the living word of God.

But let's notice the additional words in verse 3. *Obey it!* This emphasis is found through the book of Revelation, because one of the main reasons for spiritual decline was the temptation to drift away from God's word and towards the standards of the world. The same Greek word is used in Revelation 1:3: 'Blessed are those who hear the words of this prophecy and take to heart what is written in it.' And then at the close of the book, in Revelation 22:7, 'Blessed is he who keeps the words of the prophecy of this book.' The only way to recover spiritual life in Sardis – or in your life and mine – is to respond to the call to obey Jesus' words. Far from being restrictive, the truth will set us free, as day by day we seek to put into practice what we have received and heard.

And next, the call is to 'repent.' Facing up to reality is a demanding for any church which has a reputation of being alive. It is easy to fool ourselves. So the Lord Jesus calls us to repent, to deliberately renounce the drift away, and to turn back to him for forgiveness and renewal.

These then are the urgent exhortations of the living Christ. Wake up and strengthen what remains; remember and repent. Then we will find we are on our way back to genuine spiritual life. Then we will live with consistency, not hypocrisy.

3. A warning and a promise

Unexpected judgement

'But if you do not wake up, I will come like a thief, and you will not know at what time I will come to you' (v3).

Some writers wonder if the image of the unexpected arrival of Jesus, like a thief in the night, would have triggered the memory in Sardis of the occasion when the soldier in Cyrus's army crept up the cliff path with his team of colleagues, and unexpectedly the city was taken. We're familiar from the gospels with the idea of Jesus coming 'like a thief in the night.' There it is a description of his ultimate return, but probably here it is a reference to his actions now. Then he will finally come in judgement and in salvation, but now he is also constantly coming to his church, to bless and to judge. We saw in the letter to Ephesus the word of judgement that, if they do not repent, Christ would remove the lampstand from its place. So here there is a similar warning of unexpected judgement.

We might think this has been happening in the church in the West, with so many redundant church buildings turned into furniture stores, art galleries or just empty barns. And for sure, the situation in Turkey, where all seven churches once thrived, is not an encouraging one. The message is clear: don't be complacent, don't be over-confident. 'He who has an ear, let him hear what the Spirit says.' But there is not only a warning, but a promise.

Eternal security

In fact there are three promises, or three images which underline the security of every church and every believer who turns to Jesus, who listens to his word through the Spirit.

First in verse 4: 'They will walk with me, dressed in white, for they are worthy.' One of the contributory factors to the wealth of Sardis was its clothing industry. So the reference in verse 4 to soiled clothes would have been a reminder once again of reputation and reality. It was a city of clothing factories and laundries, full of respectable people who were well dressed and sustained an untarnished image. Yet in reality the Christians wore garments that were soiled and shoddy. But as we've seen, a small minority had resisted the seductive appeal of the world. Jesus says that they would wear white clothes, which is a picture is of purity. Because of Jesus Christ they are made clean.

The second image of acceptance and fellowship with God is the phrase in verse 4, 'They will walk with me.' The reward to those who overcome is companionship with God. And this is a clear difference between nominal and true religion. It describes open and intimate fellowship with Jesus himself.

The third image of security is in verse 5: our names will be in the book of life, and Christ will confess our name before his Father and the angels. The serious message to Sardis was that it was entirely possible to have a reputation for being alive, but still to have no entry in God's book of life. In other words, we don't belong. A name can be on a church register or membership list without ever being on God's register, in his book of life. But the promise to the one who overcomes is particularly strong: the Greek sentence has a double negative: 'I will never, never, by any means, blot out his name from the book of life.' That is our security as we trust Jesus, as we honour and confess his name. And how is this possible? Let's remember who it is that speaks this uncomfortable yet necessary message. He is described in verse 1 as the one who holds us in his hands, the one who makes the Spirit available to us.

Wholehearted commitment

by Jonathan Lamb

Revelation 3:14-22

Introduction

A short while ago I met a Christian leader from Kosovo. Before he was a Christian he ran various businesses, owned several shops, and became quite wealthy. He was also a body builder, and was most famous for being the Yugoslav weight-lifting champion. Then came the invasion of Kosovo. He was forced to evacuate his shops and his home, he was beaten up and his family was taken off as refugees to Albania. Eventually he found them and, when he returned to Kosovo, and looked for his shops, they were destroyed. He looked for his houses, but they were burnt down. But in both Albania and Kosovo he met Christians who helped him eventually to come to faith in Christ. Now he's serving the churches in Kosovo and beyond. And as he told me his story through a translator, he concluded by saying: 'I had nothing, but now I've found everything. The Lord is my life.'

Mother Theresa once said: 'You will never know that Jesus is all you need until Jesus is all you have.'

This, the last of the seven letters, confronts us with one final tragedy that can afflict the church. To introduce that, let me ask a few basic questions. If you were asked, 'What is Christianity?' how would you reply? At its simplest we would say: Christianity is Christ. 'What is a Christian?' A Christian is a person united to Christ. And 'What is a church?' A church is a community where Christ is at the centre. So the critical issue in the Christian life relates to our commitment to him, our dependence on Jesus Christ.

The tragedy in Laodicea was that the church lived as though Jesus didn't matter. The letter is introduced with a description of Jesus in verse 14: 'To the angel of the church in Laodicea write, "These are the words of the Amen, the faithful and true witness, the ruler of God's creation."'

'Amen.' That's a word which means it is true, it is certain. It is often used by John in his Gospel, when he quotes Jesus saying, 'Amen, Amen', or 'Truly, truly.' Jesus is implying that you can be absolutely certain about what he is saying. More than that, Jesus is himself the 'Amen', he is God's 'Yes' to everything which God has promised. He is the rock solid foundation for our lives and for our churches. We are completely dependent on him. 'The ruler of God's creation': everything has been brought into being though him. Every breath we take, every beat of our heart, every aspect of our life is because of him. It is impossible to exist without the Ruler of God's creation, Jesus himself. He is our life. So there is the letter head: this letter comes from Jesus himself, the Source and the Sustainer of our lives.

And what does Jesus have to say to Laodicea? There are three themes.

1. A sickening condition

'I know your deeds, that you are neither hot nor cold. I wish you were one or the other! So, because you are lukewarm – neither hot nor cold – I am about to spit you out of my mouth' (v15).

It's metaphorical language of course, but we understand it well enough. And the church in Laodicea would too. It was probably an allusion to the hot springs not far away in Hierapolis, which travelled across the plateau to appear opposite Laodicea as springs. By the time the water reached the city it was lime-laden and tepid. For anyone hoping for refreshment on a hot day, it was revolting. Lukewarm liquids are not only tasteless but positively *distasteful*. And Jesus' words here are an expression of disgust. I am about to spit you out of my mouth. I'm nauseated by the way you are living. Christ's verdict is that they are utterly useless. Unlike cold water which is refreshing, and hot water springs which have healing properties, lukewarm water is of no value at all. And Jesus didn't want a church like this. 'I am sick when I think about it, I am nauseated.'

What had gone wrong? Why this response from the risen Christ? In essence, they were trying to live without him. And it's a common condition. There are many people who name the name of Christ, and yet really keep him at a distance, people who like to be known as Christians and yet who also want to keep one foot in the world. Such Christians are trying to live two lives. They are half hearted, because they are double-minded. Jesus Christ, the Amen, the Ruler of creation, calls us to be totally dependent on him and wholeheartedly committed to him. So why were they lukewarm?

2. A selfish cause

As we read the letter we can identify three characteristics of the church in Laodicea.

Self satisfied

'You say, I am rich; I have acquired wealth and do not need a thing' (v17).

Many writers highlight that Laodicea in the first century was famous for three things. First, it was a banking centre: it stood at a significant point on the trading routes of the day and so it was a great commercial and financial centre. The historians tell us, for example, that when Cicero travelled to the east he would use the equivalent of his credit card at Laodicea. It was 'the Zurich of Asia Minor.' But with that great wealth came a spirit of independence. Writers often comment on the well known response of the city to an earthquake in AD61 which devastated the city. The local city council determined they would rebuild the city without the help of the state.

Not only that, it was a medical centre: the city was well known for its famous medical school, including one of its local products, an eye powder which was exported in tablet form, ground down and applied to weak or ailing eyes. And it was also a clothing centre. The sheep on the hills around Laodicea were famous for their soft, black wool, and one of the reasons for the city's wealth was related to a prosperous clothing industry with a big export market. They produced a range of tunics from the glossy black wool for which the city became famous for many centuries.

The church of course, had come to faith, had seen its need of Jesus, but little by little the insidious influence of the city in which they lived sucked them back. They became comfortable, complacent, easy-going, lukewarm. So you can understand why the Christians might have caught the spirit of the city. 'You say, I am rich . . . and have need of nothing' (v17). It's an attitude of smug self-satisfaction.

Self centred

In several of the letters, Christ's verdict highlights something critical that is missing from the life of the church. In Ephesus, love had gone: 'You have forsaken your first love.' In Sardis, life had gone: 'You have a reputation for being alive, but you are dead.' And in Laodicea, it's the most serious of all. The Lord had gone. How do we know? Because he is outside. 'Here I am! I stand at the door and knock' (v20). The Laodicean church was living in its own self-contained, self-sufficient world. They were trying to live as if Jesus didn't matter; they kept him at arm's length. There was no wholehearted commitment to Jesus – he was outside the door.

I saw someone wearing a T shirt the other day with the slogan: 'Today is all about me.' How boring is that! It's part of what we call the 'Me' culture. He probably uses Microsoft ME edition. And it can influence Christians too. It can produce a self-centred church. We effectively say to Jesus, 'We can manage, thanks. We're OK.' Self-satisfied and self centred. But the sickness is worse still.

Self-deceived

'You say I am rich . . . But you do not realize that you are wretched, pitiful, poor, blind and naked' (v17).

The risen Christ looks at such a situation and sees what is really happening, just as he did with Sardis. 'You don't realize,' Jesus says. You think there is nothing wrong, but in reality you are spiritually sick. Notice the way Jesus exposes that malaise. 'You are wretched, pitiful, poor, blind and naked.' They are well chosen words, given the prominent features of the city that we've mentioned. You might think you are a wealthy community, with prosperous trading and high-flying finance and banking, but in reality you are poor. It's the opposite of what we saw when we looked at Smyrna, when Jesus said, 'I know your afflictions and your poverty – yet you are rich' (Rev. 2:9). To the community with its medical and clothing industries: 'you are blind and naked.' That's the tragedy of this spiritual sickness. We don't know it. We are self deceived. Perhaps that's why in verse 20 the image is of Jesus patiently standing at the door, knocking. We can't hear him.

Self-satisfied, self-centred, self-deceived. It's a tragedy for any church or any Christian to be living like this. But like all seven letters, there is a response from Christ, a word of hope and of promise. The passage shows us not just a sickening condition and a selfish cause, but a saving cure.

3. A saving cure

The way back to wholehearted commitment involves three things.

Christ's love

This is what he says to the *self-deceived*. 'Those whom I love I rebuke and discipline. So be earnest and repent' (v19). We might be surprised to read it, after what Jesus has said to the church – to people he can't stomach! But this is what he says to us: I discipline those whom I love. And if the Lord has been at work convicting us this week, then he has not yet spewed us out of his mouth. He loves us and he longs that we should change. His love for us compels him to chasten, to rebuke and to discipline. Maybe as he walks among the lamp-stands, there are some of us who have grown lukewarm and who need to hear his words: be earnest and repent.

We need to recognise that, although we have received God's grace, we have cheapened it by keeping Jesus at arm's length, living as though the gospel doesn't really matter. So we must respond with seriousness – be earnest and repent. And the two words are in two different tenses. We must repent at once, and then we must continue to be fired up with zeal for the Lord Jesus. We need to turn away from the complacency of our easy-going Christianity, and commit ourselves to live our lives fully for him. The pathway to wholehearted commitment begins with confronting our self deception.

Christ's invitation

This is what he says to the *self-satisfied*. 'I counsel you to buy from me gold refined in the fire, so that you can become rich, and white clothes to wear, so you can cover your shameful nakedness; and salve to put on your eyes, so you can see' (v18).

First, notice where we will find the true spiritual resources we need. Jesus says 'buy *from me*.' They were saying, 'I am rich, I do not need a thing.' But they must come to find their sufficiency in Jesus Christ.

Jesus explained in the Beatitudes, the manifesto of the kingdom of God, that his values were not of this world. He has stepped into life's window and swopped the price tags round, so that those things which were of great value were now of little value, and those things of little value were now of great value. And his first Beatitude states the key issue: 'Blessed are those who know their need of God', who in their deepest evaluation of themselves, know their spiritual bankruptcy. And that is what Jesus is implying here. They might have imagined themselves to be rich, to be well dressed, to have 20/20 vision. Yet in reality they are poor and blind and naked.

So, to the poor, Christ offers gold refined in the fire. They are naked, but Christ offers them clothes to cover their shameful nakedness. They are blind, but Christ offers them eye-salve to put on their eyes, so that they can see. They needn't trust their banks, or their clothing industry or their medical school. They don't need the passing glories of this world. They need Christ himself.

The words of Jesus to come 'buy from him' remind us of the words the Lord spoke through Isaiah in chapter 55. There is a paradox expressed in the invitation. 'Come buy wine and milk without money and without cost.' The invitation is to those who have no resources to buy what they need. Yet this spiritual sustenance can be received without price. Isaiah – and the risen Christ in Revelation 3 – are talking about a gift of God's grace, because the price has already been paid. The gospel of God's grace is an invitation to the needy, an invitation that asks of us nothing other than repentance. That's true when we become Christians and it's true right through our Christian lives. And paradoxically, it's why so many people reject it. It's why the message of the cross is mocked as foolish. We would prefer to contribute to our own salvation. It's the reason for the popularity of New Age, because you don't need a Saviour from outside. You explore within, you believe in yourself.

It's an extremely common attitude. It's the religious attitude. I'm going to heaven because basically I'm good and even if I fail, I can make up for it. The parable about the Pharisee and tax collector was told by Jesus, Luke says, 'to some who were confident of their own righteousness and looked down on everyone else.' The tax collector had the attitude that Jesus looks for: 'God have mercy on me a sinner.' It is not the smug, self-satisfied Laodicean conviction that 'I have need of nothing.' It is the person who knows their need of God. We must recognise that he is all we need.

So the saving cure is first, *Christ's love*, confronting our self-deception. Second, *Christ's invitation* to receive all we need, confronting our self-satisfaction.

Christ's fellowship

Thirdly, this is what he says to the *self-centred*. 'Here I am! I stand at the door and knock. If anyone hears my voice and opens the door, I will come in and eat with him and he with me' (v20).

It is an extraordinary verse. The person who responds to Jesus' voice and opens the door – that is, the person who turns away from self-centred living, and sees their need of Jesus – will experience his fellowship and know his friendship. The picture in verse 20 reminds us of an evening meal in a Mediterranean country. In Britain we're used to fast food and TV meals, but in many countries an evening meal is not just for eating, but also for company, for friendship. It's a leisurely time with good food and good friends. And Jesus longs for us to open the door, so that we eat with him and he with us. This is not in the first instance an evangelistic appeal, calling people to become Christians. The Laodiceans had already responded to Christ. But they had gradually nudged him out, shifted him from centre stage, replaced him with other things.

So the invitation of verse 20 – the call to welcome Jesus into every part of our life – is a call to wholehearted allegiance. And it is a very personal appeal. Although it is addressed to a church, it is a word to each of us. 'If *anyone* hears my voice . . .' And it is a reminder not only of our present fellowship with Christ, but also anticipates that heavenly banquet to which John refers later in Revelation.

There is one further aspect of his invitation, a final promise which is even more remarkable. We will not only share his fellowship, but we will share his rule. 'To him who overcomes, I will give the right to sit with me on my throne, just as I overcame and sat down with my Father on his throne' (v21).

This is Jesus' message to the church. He exposes a *sickening condition* with a *selfish cause* and presents us with a *saving cure* through his love, his invitation and his fellowship. In essence it is a call to wholehearted discipleship, a call to repent, to open the door and to receive all we need from him. That is the way back from the sickening condition of lukewarmness. So let me ask: have you heard him knocking? If you have, don't leave him outside. We are confronted with that fundamental choice. What – or who – are you going to live for? We can live in a half-hearted, self-centred way – the kind of life which is so distasteful to Jesus that it runs the risk of his rejection. Or we can be a wholehearted disciple, trusting him, dependent on him, submitting to him, in fellowship with him, and eventually reigning with him.

I love Jesus' twin parables of the farmer and the pearl collector. The farmer is ploughing one day when he discovers some buried treasure. So he covers it up, and sells everything he has in order to buy the field. Or the pearl collector who comes across the last thing in pearls – the smoothest, purest pearl. He sells his house, his servants, his entire pearl collection, in order to buy that one pearl. And Jesus tells the stories to show that these men, in selling everything they had, in giving up everything else, were not viewing it as hardship or sacrifice. They did it 'out of joy.' It was reckless and wholehearted, because they knew that the goal of securing the treasure, of buying the pearl, was worth it. So Jesus says: Give your life for something worthwhile, for something that will last forever. Jim Elliott, the missionary martyr, is well known for a powerful statement: 'He is no fool who gives what he cannot keep to gain what he cannot lose.'

'He who has an ear, let him hear what the Spirit says to the churches.'

Keswick 2006

CDs, DVDs, Tapes, videos and books

All talks recorded at Keswick 2006 plus many more audio and video recordings from the Keswick Convention dating back to 1957 can be ordered from www.essentialchristian.com
http://www.essentialchristian.com
Catalogues and price lists of audio and video recordings of the Keswick Convention platform and seminar ministry, including much that is not included in this book, can be obtained from

ICC, Silverdale Road, Eastbourne
Sussex, BN20 7AB
Tel: 01323 643341/Fax: 01323 649240
www.essentialchristian.com

Details of DVDs, videos, CDs and cassettes and downloads of selected sessions can also be obtained from the above address. Some previous annual Keswick volumes (all published by STL/Authentic Media) can be obtained from:

The Keswick Convention Centre
Skiddaw Street, Keswick, Cumbria, CA12 4BY

Tel: 01768780075
www.keswickministries.org

or from your local Christian bookseller or direct from the publishers, Authentic Media, 9 Holdom Avenue, Bletchley, Milton Keynes, MK1 1QR. Tel: 0800834315
or from www.wesleyowen.com

Keswick 2007

Week 1 14th – 20th July
Week 2 21st – 27th July
Week 3 28th July – 4th August

The annual Keswick Convention takes place in the heart of the English Lake District, an area of outstanding natural beauty. It offers an unparalleled opportunity to listen to gifted Bible exposition, meeting Christians from all over the world and enjoying the grandeur of God's creation. Each of the three weeks has a series of morning Bible readings, and then a varied programme of seminars, lectures, literary lunches, prayer meetings, concerts, drama and other events throughout the day, with evening meetings that combine worship and teaching. There is also a full programme for children and young people, and a special track for those with learning difficulties which takes place in week 2. K2, the interactive track for those in their twenties and thirties, also takes place in week 2.

The theme for Keswick 2007 is *Unshackled? Living in outrageous grace.*
The Bible readings will be given by:
Alec Motyer (week 1) on Exodus
Steve Brady (week 2) on Galatians
Alistair Begg (week 3) on the Ten Commandments

Other confirmed speakers are Dotha Blackwood, Clive Calver, Dave Fenton, Liam Goligher, Chris Green, Jonathan Lamb, Peter Maiden, Simon Manchester, John Stott and Rico Tice.

For further information, please contact: The Operations Manager, Keswick Convention Centre, Skiddaw Street, Keswick, Cumbria, CA12 4BY. Tel: 01768780075

Email:info@keswickministries.org
Website: www.keswickministries.org